Rats' Tales

Carol Ann Duffy was born in Glasgow and grew up in Stafford. She won the 1993 Whitbread Award for Poetry and the Forward Prize for best collection for *Mean Time*. *The World's Wife* received the E. M. Forster Award in America, while *Rapture* won the T. S. Eliot Prize in 2005. She is Professor of Contemporary Poetry at Manchester Metropolitan University. Her most recent volumes are *New and Collected Poems for Children* (2009) and *The Bees* (2011), which won the Costa Poetry Award. This is her fifth collaboration with Melly Still. Carol Ann Duffy is Poet Laureate.

Melly Still has worked as a director, choreographer, designer and adaptor for many companies, including the National Theatre, Glyndebourne, the RSC, Bristol Old Vic, Hampstead and the Young Vic. She has been nominated for Olivier and Tony awards (best director and best design). Her work has travelled throughout the UK, Europe, Scandinavia, the Far East the US and Broadway. *Rats' Tales* is the latest of many collaborations with Carol Ann Duffy.

Rats' Tales

told by
CAROL ANN DUFFY

adapted for the stage by
MELLY STILL

faber and faber

First published in 2012
by Faber and Faber Limited
74–77 Great Russell Street
London WC1B 3DA

Typeset by Country Setting, Kingsdown, Kent CT14 8ES
Printed and bound by CPI Group (UK) Ltd, Croydon, CR0 4YY

Introduction © Melly Still, 2012
Dramatisations © Melly Still, 2012
Stories © Carol Ann Duffy, 2012

'The Lost Happy Endings' was first published
in a different version with illustrations by Jane Ray
(*The Lost Happy Endings*, Bloomsbury, 2006)

'A Little Girl', 'Invisible' and 'The Stolen Childhood' were published
in earlier forms in *The Stolen Childhood and Other Dark Fairy Tales*
(Puffin, 2003)

A CIP record for this book is available from the British Library

ISBN 978-0-571-29904-1

2 4 6 8 10 9 7 5 3 1

Contents

Introduction

This collection is inspired by Carol Ann Duffy's retelling of *The Pied Piper of Hamelin*. She wanted to write a version for the stage and relate it to other tales involving rats, tales that unpick our relationship to rats, to the dark, grimy, fidgety place they occupy in our imaginations. Perhaps through dwelling in this place, we'd be less repelled. As the two of us considered the stories, another more pressing theme began to emerge, especially when we thought about including in the mix some original fairy tales by Carol Ann. The theme linking the stories is stolen childhood – as much about growing old, or the transition from childhood to adulthood, or the fateful decisions adults make on behalf of their children, as about children mysteriously disappearing.

Some of the stories in the *Rats' Tales* collection have sister texts, versions adapted for the stage that maintain their core form and remain faithful to the original narrative voice. Description becomes stage direction, leaving the bare events to spring from Carol Ann's unique wordsmithery. I write this a few days before we begin rehearsals and I imagine the text will undergo some revision but, above all, my wish is that in performance the intimate relationship between teller and listener remains intact in order to simply and directly communicate these remarkable tales. Some of the stories in this collection remain in prose alone. Though they formed a significant part of our early musing we had to decide on the right mix for the stage.

The Pied Piper of Hamelin, our lead story, derives from an historical account of the disappearance of the children of Hamelin in the thirteenth century. Why they disappeared remains a mystery. Some theorists suggest an accident such as a landslide or an outbreak of the plague, the piper representing a medieval figure of death. Communal dancing mania wasn't uncommon in Europe after attacks of the plague, which might account for the children's ecstatic dancing. Other theorists suggest the children, led by a pipe-playing recruiter, emigrated to found their own villages during a period of Eastern European colonisation. A manuscript (*c.* 1440–1450) originally written in Latin verse gives an account of the event:

> In the year of 1284, on the day of Saints John and Paul on
>   the 26th of June,
> 130 children born in Hamelin were seduced
> By a piper, dressed in all kinds of colours,
> And lost at the place of execution near the koppen [*hills*].

As a true-ish story with an irredeemably bleak ending it breaks the mould of fairy tales. For the stage production, which we hope will strike deeply into the hearts of all ages, this presented myself and Anna Fleischle (the designer for *Rats' Tales*) with the challenge of providing an experience that wouldn't deter our younger spectators. We begin by assuming that every member of the audience regardless of age is as sophisticated as the next but assimilating the blunt consequences of not paying the piper might be an unwelcome challenge for an eight-year-old. The answer came after a visit to the Royal Exchange Theatre, Manchester, who commissioned the project. It's the building itself, vast and Victorian, originally constructed for the exchange of cotton and textiles but now housing a 1970s pod construction, that inspired us. It feels as if a sci-fi circus has come to town and when you see work performed there, the pod-within-a-hall atmosphere never quite disappears.

Far from this being a problem, we decided to embrace its peculiarity and artifice. We pictured paths within the pod spilling into the hall and beyond into the street; security cameras capturing action in the hall and relaying to screens within the pod. We imagined the usually anonymous quick-changing areas becoming dressing rooms, inviting roaming audience members to peer behind the scenes before the show; and rats (played by local children) inhabiting the hall as the audience arrive and enticing them into their seats with a chant.

The idea of a troupe coming to town took hold. It's as if some players from Hamelin (leaning on the story's medieval origins) have decided to travel the world and tell their story (perhaps they are the once lost children, now grown).

At the end of the story the townsfolk are left to grapple with grief and remorse. This beleaguered community begin to play out their memories and experience through the sharing of more tales, in turns mysterious, haunting, lyrical and raucous. The unfolding dramas have an unexpected effect: the community are touched by the stories, relishing the simple voice that seeks to communicate their love and their loss. Quietly and gradually they find themselves transformed from griefstricken to embracing joy once more. Eventually the children return. Perhaps they are part of the rat's dream that inhabits the final story. Perhaps their return represents the parents' reconciliation with loss. Perhaps the children were only playing and were enticed back by magical storytelling.

Melly Still
October 2012

Rats' Tales was first performed in this dramatisation at the Royal Exchange Theatre, Manchester, on 29 November 2012. The cast was as follows:

Woodcutter Hiran Abeysekera
Teacher Meline Danielewicz
Seamstress Katherine Manners
Pied Piper Michael Mears
Politician Dan Milne
Priest Jack Tarlton
Poet Emily Wachter
Cook Kelly Williams

Musicians Tom Thorp, Rosemary Toll

Director Melly Still
Designer Anna Fleischle
Lighting Designer Paul Anderson
Composer and Sound Designer Dave Price
Video Design Soup Collective
Associate Director Andrew Barry
Assistant Director Holly Race Roughan
Costume Supervisor Ilona Karas

For Ella, Felix, Olive and Iris
with love from their Mothers

RATS' TALES

the dramatisations by

MELLY STILL

The Pied Piper of Hamelin

Priest A long time ago in the town of Hamelin, which is still there, there was an invasion of rats the like of which it is impossible for us to imagine, but we will try.

Seamstress These rats were dirty great black things which ran as they pleased in broad daylight through the streets and swarmed all over the houses so that folk couldn't put their hand or foot down without touching something furry.

Priest When dressing in the morning they found rats in their underpants and petticoats, in their hats, boots, the teacher's briefcase.

Teacher One poor citizen had found two rats playing in her brassiere.

Priest When anyone wanted a bite to eat, the rats had been there first!

Cook The Cook, for example, was always going into her larder and finding that the rats had eaten the cheese or sucked the eggs or nibbled the bread or gnawed the rind off the best bacon. The Cook had a good moan about it to the Priest . . .

Priest . . . who agreed with her, because he had found rats in the pockets of his cassock, and had had his King James Bible chewed from Genesis to Revelations.

Woodcutter In fact, there was nowt left of his Holy Candle but the wick!

3

Priest The Priest had a right old bitch about it with the Poet, who agreed with him . . .

Poet . . . because she couldn't write poetry any more on account of the noise. As soon as it got dark, the rats set to work, nibbling away from cellar to garret.

Everywhere, in the ceilings, in the floors, in the cupboards, at the doors, there was a scamper and a rummage, and such a furious noise of gimlets, pincers and saws, that the Poet was a nervous wreck!

Seamstress So the townsfolk agreed to march to the Town Hall and find the Politician to demand that something was done about the bloody rats.

Politician (*calming the townsfolk*) We are all in this together. I will launch an Official Inquiry.

Uproar. Everyone plonks themselves down on their bottoms and refuses to budge until the Politician comes up with a better idea.

Seamstress Well, they sat there from noon till dusk . . .

Politician . . . while the Politican consulted his Moral Compass . . . and looked at his Legacy . . . and mentioned his Mandate . . .

Priest . . . when there arrived in the town a man with an unusual face who played a pipe.

He is an odd, gawky person, very weatherbeaten.

Piper (*singing*)
If you live, you'll see
This is me –
I was born to be
The Rat-catcher!

The Politician approaches warily, the Townsfolk retreat.

If you make it worth my while, I will get rid of all your rats, right down to the last one.

Seamstress He's not from round here!

Woodcutter He might trick us!

Cook We can't trust him!

Uproar. The Politician tries to calm the voters.

Politician But the Politician knew a potential vote-winner when he saw one! He was determined that it was high time everyone went home and stopped blaming him for the rats.

(Turning to the Piper.) I give you my word of honour, Piper, that you will be properly rewarded, should you succeed in ridding our town of rats. How much do you charge?

Piper By midnight tonight, I shall remove every rat from this place, if you promise to pay me one gold sovereign for each rat.

Townsfolk One gold sovereign for each rat! But that will come to millions of pounds!

Politician Despite the grumbling of the people, the Politician was not for turning.

He shakes hands with the Piper and gives him a beaming smile.

I guarantee to pay you one gold sovereign for every rat with the taxpayers' own money.

Piper I will start this evening when the moon rises. Leave the streets empty, but look out of your windows, it will be an interesting event.

Priest And so, at about nine o'clock that night, the Pied Piper reappeared by the Town Hall, back to the Church, and as the moon rose, he began to play on his pipe.

At first the music is slow and dreamy, gentle as a caress; but then it grows more and more lively as though it is saying 'Come and dance!'

Poet From the depths of the cellars and sewers . . .

Teacher . . . from the tops of the attics and garrets . . .

Cook . . . from out of the larders . . .

Seamstress . . . cupboards . . .

Woodcutter . . . wardrobes, handbags and wellingtons . . .

Politician . . . from under the beds and tables . . .

Poet . . . from every corner of every house . . .

Seamstress . . . or shop . . .

Cook . . . out came the rats!

The rats are squeezed together, a filthy flood in full flow.

Priest When the square was completely crammed, the Piper turned away and began to walk towards the river at the foot of the town.

The Piper plays wonderfully, magically. The rats follow eagerly until the Piper stops playing and points to the middle of the river where the water is flowing, swirling, foaming and whirling dangerously.

Hop hop! Hop hop!

Priest And straight away, without pausing for a moment, the rats began to jump in . . .

Poet . . . head first . . .

Cook . . . one after another . . .

Poet . . . and disappeared.

6

Priest It was almost midnight when, at the very end of the line, came a big old rat, silver with age. It was the boss of the plague.

Piper Are they all in, my old friend?

Old Rat They are all in, brother.

Piper And how many were there?

Old Rat Nine hundred and ninety thousand, nine hundred and ninety-nine.

Piper Including you?

Old Rat Including me.

Piper Then go and join them, old friend, till we meet again.

Poet Then the silver rat jumped into the river and disappeared.

Priest The Piper had kept his end of the bargain and went off to his bed at the inn.

Woodcutter And for the first time in a long, long while, the woodcutter and all the citizens of Hamelin slept peacefully through the night.

Poet And the Poet was able to start at last on a new poem.

Priest The next morning, just after nine o'clock . . .

Cook . . . the well-rested and breakfasted citizens gathered outside the Town Hall . . .

Seamstress . . . to cheer and applaud the Politician.

Piper All your rats went for a swim in the river last night and I guarantee not one will return. There were nine hundred and ninety thousand, nine hundred and

ninety-nine, at one gold sovereign a head. It is time to
count out my wages.

Politician (*smiling*) Just a moment, stranger, one
sovereign a head means one head a sovereign. Where are
the heads?

*The Taxpayers roar with laughter, the Piper shakes
with rage and his eyes burn red.*

Piper (*hissing*) The heads? If you want the heads, then
go and find them in the river!

Politician (*booming confidently*) Oh, I see! You are
refusing to keep to the terms of our arrangement. One
sovereign per head. Where are the heads?

Townsfolk (*finding courage in the crowd*) Where are the
heads? Where are the heads? Show us the heads!

Politician (*in charge once more*) Order! Order!
(*Turning to the Piper.*) We could refuse even to pay
you a penny. But we are a Big Society and you have been
of use to us. Why not accept a token ten sovereigns for
your trouble, before you leave?

Piper (*poisonously*) Keep your token ten sovereigns. If
you do not pay me, I will be paid by your children.

Politician The Rat-catcher has been caught in his own
trap!

*The Taxpayers give high-fives and slap each other on
the back laughing. The Politician enjoys his popularity.*

Pass our debt on to our children!

The parents laugh uncontrollably.

Priest The next day was a Sunday and they all went
happily to the Church, looking forward to a Sunday
lunch after Mass that hadn't been sampled by rats.

Seamstress But when everyone returned home . . .

Pause.

Cook . . . their children had gone.

Townsfolk (*distraught*) Our children! Where are our children?

Priest Then, limping from the east side of the town, came a little lame boy who was sobbing loudly and this is what he told: while all the adults were at Church, a wonderful music had started.

All the boys and girls who had been left safely at home run outside, following the magical sound to the square by the Town Hall. They find the Pied Piper there, playing his music just as he had on the night he caught all the rats.

Seamstress Then the Piper had walked quickly towards the east gate of the town as far as the foot of the mountain outside Hamelin.

The children follow, running, singing, clapping, dancing to the music.

Priest But when they got near, the mountain had opened and the Piper had gone in, still playing his music . . .

Woodcutter . . . and all the children had danced after him . . .

Cook . . . after which the mountain had closed again.

Lame Boy I was the only child left because I could not keep up with the others.

Teacher When they heard this story . . .

Woodcutter . . . they ran to the mountain.

Cook And banged at the rock till darkness . . .

9

Poet . . . searching for the opening.

Politician The Politician, who had lost three little boys and two little girls, clawed at the stone with his bare hands . . .

Seamstress . . . but it was all useless.

Pause.

Priest When night fell, the citizens had to return to Hamelin without their children, and only the cold face of the moon was witness to the dreadful sights and sounds of their grief.

The Stolen Childhood

Mother A mother lived with her young daughter. The girl was sweet-natured and lovely, but the mother had a heart that had soured and shrivelled.

Day after day, she watched her daughter as she played in the garden and the mother's blood clogged with envy as she saw the young girl chasing butterflies or turning cartwheels or singing to herself in the arms of the apple tree.

Daughter (*playing*) Salt, mustard, pepper, vinegar / He blew her a kiss then drew it in again.

Mother More than anything, I yearn to be young again.

One day, the mother, staring as usual from her window, noticed a stranger walking in the lane. He was tall and dark and as the woman gazed down at him, he glanced up and spied her. With one look he saw into her dark soul and knew what she wanted.

Stranger Come to me.

She jumps, as though a poker is stirring the burnt coals and ashes of her heart. Close up she sees that there is no kindness in his face and she shivers. He is holding a pair of sharp silver scissors.

I can give you what you most want. Take these scissors and cut the shadow from the first young person you find asleep. Then snip off your own shadow and throw it over the young person without waking them. Their youth will be yours at once and they will be as old as you are now.

Mother What must I pay you for this?

Stranger You will be my bride, on the happiest day of your life.

Mother (*a dry laugh*) The mother thought that the man was joking

But she agrees to his strange bargain and takes the scissors.

He walked rapidly away and quite soon after that he left the town.

The Mother enters the garden holding the scissors, which glitter in her hand in the sunlight.

Her young daughter is stretched out on the lawn with her straw hat over her face, fast asleep in the warm buttery sun.

Her daughter's shadow lay on the grass beside her, so cool and dark.

The Mother kneels down, silent as poison, and cuts along the whole length of the girl's shadow. A breeze blows under it and lifts it gently, but the Mother snatches at it, crumpling it up and stuffing it in her skirt pocket. It feels like the softest silk.

The mother stood and saw her own long shadow at her feet. She bent down and with a *snap!* and a *snip!* she cut it off. She lifted her heavy, leathery shadow and tossed it over the sleeping girl, then turned and ran towards the house to look in the mirror. Her step felt lighter and for the first time in years she noticed all the different smells of the garden as she ran.

The Daughter feels something heavy and sour-smelling upon her and opens her eyes in fright. It's dark. She screams and tries to jump up but her body feels stiff and strange and her back aches.

She sits up and pushes the shadow away from her and it lies in a heap like an old black coat.

Daughter How horrible!

Mother (*watching*) Her voice was different, deeper and harsher –

Daughter – not like a child's voice at all.

Mother She looked at her hands. They were like a pair of crumpled gloves, several sizes too big, the skin loose and creased over the bones.

She stands up slowly, holding the small of her back, and hears the waxy creak of her knees. Truly scared now, she hurries as fast as she can, a bit out of breath, to look in the mirror.
The Mother stands before the mirror. Both of them stare at each other in disbelief. The Mother begins to laugh, the light easy laugh of a young girl.

Look at yourself!

She pulls her daughter to the mirror.

Daughter A middle-aged face stared back from the glass, grey-haired and lined. The daughter's teeth felt strange and uncomfortable in her mouth –

She realises that they are false. She coughs.

– and the bitter taste of tobacco scalded the back of her throat.

She turns to the Mother.

How small you are, with soft hair the colour of a conker and skin as delicate as the petal of a rose.

The Mother jumps up and down and claps her hands.

Mother It worked! It worked! I am young again and *you* have all my years!

The Mother spins round and runs back into the sunshine. The Daughter falls to the floor and sobs bitterly.

Stranger Summer turned, as it has to do, into autumn and autumn soon became winter.

Daughter It was the daughter now who stood at the window, a shawl round her cold stiff bones, watching the village children throw snowballs in the field on the other side of the lane.

She wondered why her young mother never played with the others. What was the point of her mother being young at all?

Mother Youth is wasted on the young. I am young again! Young! See my skin and my eyes and my hair sparkle in the white winter light.

Daughter The mother grew tall and beautiful, and many young suitors came to the house to visit her.

Lover They brought flowers and perfume and chocolates and told her that they adored her –

Lover – and that she was the loveliest young girl in the village –

Lover – that her lips were rubies and her eyes were sapphires –

Lover – and that each little nail on the tips of her fingers was a pearl.

Mother I am in the springtime of my life. Again!

Daughter Her daughter watched the young lovers come and go from her window, but none of them so much as glanced up at the sad old woman with the dull eyes and the yellowing teeth.

Daughter One young man was handsomer and jollier than all the rest and her heart, tired as it was, would skip a beat as though it had almost remembered something, whenever she saw him.

At night she would dream that she was dancing and laughing in his arms, a girl once more. But when she woke up she was alone, brittle and aching.

As the summer passed, she noticed that the young man came more and more often to the house.

Mother On the first day of autumn her mother and the young man came before her and told her that they were to be married.

Daughter Her tired heart sank like a stone in her chest as she looked at the young man and she knew then that she loved him.

She kisses her mother.

I wish you every happiness.

Mother Oh, I will be happy. My wedding day will be the happiest day of my life. We will be married at Christmas and I will wear a dress of silver and gold.

The warm bronze voices of the bells ring across the frozen fields. The Daughter waits for the carriages to arrive. The cold bites into her bones.

Daughter (*singing*)
Winter has stolen summer's child
Ice chills her bones and breath
Cold bells toll the arrival of
Old age and death
Old age and death

Mother Here I am! How do I look?

Stranger You look good enough to eat.

The Daughter sees the shock and surprise on her Mother's face and turns to see who has spoken. A tall man with a mean face and fierce eyes appears from nowhere and stares intensely at the bride.

Our carriage will soon be here.

Mother Our carriage? You must be mistaken!

The colour drains from her face until she is paler than the late white roses she carries in her hands.

Stranger (*impatiently*) Come. You know very well what is to happen today.

Mother (*trembling*) Today is to be the happiest day of my life. I am to marry the young man who loves me.

Stranger You are to marry me, my beauty, and you can forget about love. Come!

Mother Marry you? You?

She laughs hysterically.
An ebony carriage arrives drawn by black horses steaming and snorting. The Mother is crying and shaking with fear. She clutches her daughter's arm.

Daughter Who is he?

Stranger Get into the carriage!

Mother (*wild with terror*) No! No! You can't make me!

Daughter Who is he? Tell me!

Stranger For the last time, get into the carriage.

The Mother looks into his eyes and sees all the badness of this world and the next. She shakes her head.
The Stranger gives a twisted smile and stares hard at the bride.

You have broken your promise. Put your hand in the pocket of your dress.

The Mother pulls out a small piece of crumpled black silk. She gives a little scream and drops it. It floats to the ground and lands at her daughter's feet.
The Stranger pulls off his coat and the Daughter sees that it is the old black coat that had nearly suffocated her when she was a child. With a quick movement the Stranger throws it over her mother, completely covering her lovely gold and silver dress.

Mother (*screaming*) Don't! I'll come! I'll come!

Stranger Too late.

The horses toss their heads and the Stranger in the ebony carriage gallops away.

Mother Come back!

The clatter of hooves fades into the distance. The Mother flings away the coat.

Help me! What am I to do?

Her daughter stares in horror. The Mother's dress hangs in tattered grey rags. Her hair has turned white and clumps of it have fallen from her head. Her mouth has shrunk inwards in a small wrinkled O of disappointment. Her body shrivels and stoops till she looks like a question mark asking, 'Why? Why? Why?' Her voice when she speaks is the dusty croak of a crone.

Why do you stare at me?

She clutches at her throat and gapes at her daughter. Colour is flooding back into the Daughter's hair, and the girl is smiling with perfect white teeth.

17

Daughter What is happening to me?

She hears the light music of her own voice and she laughs with delight.

Mother! I am myself again!

She feels her young lungs breathing easily and her heart opens like a flower. The Mother is bent double coughing and cursing. The Bridegroom, out of breath, runs in looking for the bride. He glances curiously at the old woman, but as soon as he sees the girl he has eyes only for her.

Daughter Your bride has gone.

There is a strange noise and they both turn to see the old black coat lying in a heap. There is no sign of the mother, but a sudden gust of wind blows a handful of ashes, grey and gritty, over the fields.

Your bride has gone for ever.

Bridegroom My bride was lovely but you are truly the most beautiful girl I have ever seen in my life.

Daughter The girl looked down at her hands and saw the light of youth that glowed under her skin and she felt the force and energy of life itself rise up from the tingling tips of her toes so that all she wanted to do was run.

(*Laughing and taking to her heels.*) Catch me if you can!

With a shout, laughing, he chases her, never quite catching her.

A Little Girl

Narrator 1 A Little Girl lived with her little family in a Doll's House.

Narrator 2 There was Little Grandma, who had her own room at the top of the house.

Narrator 3 There was Little Grandad, who dozed in a rocking chair in front of the fire all day, even in summer.

Narrator 2 There was Little Mother, who spent most of her time in the kitchen cooking.

Narrator 3 And there was Little Twin, the Little Girl's twin sister, who shared her bedroom and slept above the Little Girl in the top bunk.

Narrator 1 Every morning, the little family would eat breakfast together in the kitchen and Little Mother would serve tiny boiled eggs in teeny egg cups and the weeniest glasses of orange juice.

Narrator 2 After breakfast, Little Grandma would climb up the stairs to her room, sit on a little chair and stare out of the window.

Narrator 3 Little Grandad rocked himself slowly to sleep in front of the orange and crimson fire while Little Mother tidied away the breakfast things; and the Little Girl and her Little Twin went to the drawing room to play on the little upright piano or read wee books or dance together.

Narrator 1 The afternoons ticked away, the two children throwing a red ball between them, the size of a berry.

Every day was the same and whenever the Little Girl asked to go outside her mother shushed her or her grandparents tutted or her sister shook her head.

At night, when the house grew dark, tiny lamps came on in the Doll's House and the little family sat together round the fire until it was time for bed. Then the Little Girl lay in her bottom bunk with her eyes wide open, listening to the thick deep silence of the darkness.

One morning, the Little Girl looked across at her Little Twin and noticed that she seemed smaller. The Little Girl thought that perhaps she was imagining this, but her own tiny black shoes no longer fitted and she had to go about the house barefooted since they were her only pair.

Narrator 2 When she sat down for breakfast, she found that her chair was too small for her and her knees scraped on the underside of the kitchen table. She was still hungry after she'd eaten her boiled egg and toast and still thirsty after she'd drained her weeny glass of orange juice, but nobody else seemed to notice these things, so the Little Girl said nothing.

Narrator 3 Later, when she asked whether she might go outside, her mother shushed her and her grandparents tutted and her sister shook her head. That night, as she lay in her bunk, her feet poked out from under her blankets and her head pressed hard against the wall behind her pillow, so she gathered her bedclothes together and stretched out on the floor till morning came.

Narrator 1 When the light from outside arrived, she sat up to discover that her head was at the same height as her Little Twin's bunk bed.

Narrator 2 Little Twin started to cry as she looked at her sister's large, pale face, a breathing moon, then she ran downstairs to the kitchen, calling for Little Mother.

Narrator 3 From then on, the Little Girl grew apart from the rest of her family. They looked at her strangely as she squeezed herself through the little doors of the Doll's House or stooped and knelt to avoid banging her head on the ceilings.

Narrator 1 They complained bitterly when they found that she had eaten the entire contents of their little fridge to satisfy her hunger. They whispered to themselves when she knocked over the furniture as she passed.

Curled in the attic, the largest space in the house, the Little Girl heard the fierce squeaks of her family's voices far below. She lifted her arms above her head, carefully raised the red-tiled roof of the Doll's House and climbed outside.

Now that she stands at her full height, the Little Girl sees that she is as tall as the Doll's House. She puts her eye to the glass of her grandmother's room. Little Grandma sits in her chair staring out through her window, still and unblinking.

Little Girl Grandma looks just like a wax doll! My sister is still reading the same page of that wee book!

Narrator 2 The Little Girl's eyes filled with tears which fell and splashed against the window like rain.

She stretches out and leans on her elbow to peep through the kitchen window where Little Mother is standing at the table ready to tidy away the breakfast things.

Little Girl Oh Mother, would you put on your teeny hat and weeny coat and walk out of the kitchen, along the hall and out through the front door?

No reply.

Narrator 2 That night, the Little Girl lay down on the floor outside the Doll's House. She could see the tiny lights go out inside the house as she drifted away into sleep.

Narrator 1 When she awoke, there was a bed with plump pillows –

Little Girl – and a pair of shoes that were just the right size.

Delicious cooking smells. Her Tall Mother enters and smiles at her.

Narrator 2 / Tall Mother Breakfast is in the garden!

Little Girl And there is the whole wide wonderful world stretching endlessly away.

Narrator 3 So the girl grew and grew and the Doll's House stayed in the corner of her bedroom. She peeped in through its windows at first, but soon she forgot to do this –

Little Girl – for she had her own big windows now and she could see the stars.

Narrator 1 In time, the Doll's House was packed away and forgotten.

Little Girl She became a woman and had her own family . . .

Narrator 1 And, though she had her troubles from time to time as everyone does, she was very happy for many years.

Narrator 2 One day, the woman looked in the mirror.

Little Girl I have become old.

Narrator 3 In the autumn she went up to the attic to store some apples that needed ripening.

Little Girl She saw, tucked away in a corner, the old Doll's House.

Narrator 3 She knelt before it and peered in through one of the upstairs windows. Little Grandma was sitting in her chair, staring sightlessly out. The woman's heart gave a horrible lurch and her breath came out in a gasp, covering the window with a fine mist.

Narrator 2 She rubbed at the glass with a corner of her sleeve and Little Grandma stared right through her just as before.

Little Girl Little Grandma! Here I am!

Narrator 1 She looked into the window of her old bedroom and saw that both the little bunk beds were empty, so she crouched lower and peeped into the drawing-room window. She tapped on the pane with her fingernail.

Little Girl Little Twin, look up! Oh, still on the same page! Wakey wakey, Little Grandad!

Narrator 3 Little Twin didn't look up from her wee book and Little Grandad slept on.

Little Girl Mother, where are you?

Narrator 2 The woman felt herself shrinking with longing and regret. She moved her head till it was level with the kitchen window. Little Mother was standing at the table as she always had.

Little Girl Mother, it is me! Open the door! Please, Little Mother! My heart is brimming with love for you.

Narrator 3 Without thinking, she banged hard on the glass with her fists. Then Little Mother was waving and smiling at her and ran down the hall to fling open the door. And she felt her Little Twin's tiny hands in hers, pulling her inside, and heard the small excited clucks of Little Grandma and Little Grandad as they walked towards her.

Narrator 2 The door closed behind her with a small click.

Narrator 1 That night the Little Girl stood at her bedroom window as her little family slept. Outside the Doll's House, planets glowed and shone like giant apples far out in the endless universe.

Invisible

Mother This lad lived happily with his parents on the edge of a village in the very last cottage before the forest began.

His mother worked in the woods collecting chestnuts, hazelnuts and walnuts.

His father laboured as a woodcutter, chopping up wood for furniture and fuel.

But one terrible day the father had an accident in the forest and died. The lad and his mother wept as the father was buried in a coffin nailed together from wood he had cut down himself. They grieved for two winters, but when spring came again, the lad's mother met a new man and married him.

Boy When his mother and stepfather came home from their honeymoon, the lad was waiting for them.

Mother His mother ran to him and kissed him . . .

Stepfather . . . but his stepfather looked straight through him as though he wasn't there.

Boy When bedtime came, the lad kissed his mother goodnight, but when he looked to do the same to his stepfather . . .

Stepfather . . . the man ignored him and carried on reading his book.

Boy The lad climbed the stairs and sat on his narrow bed. He looked out at the forest where his father had died, where alder, ash, aspen, willow, beech, cherry, poplar, oak, birch, hawthorn, hazel, juniper, lime, rowan, pine, elm, yew and his father all whispered to him in the darkness. Afraid, he closed his ears until his sorrow hardened and his tears were small glass stones in his eyes.

Mother The lad slept late and when he came down for breakfast, his mother had already left to collect nuts in the forest.

Stepfather His stepfather was writing letters at the table and barely glanced at him when he sat down with his milk and his bread roll.

The Boy eats in silence, conscious of the small slurps he makes as he drinks. He is a handsome man, unsmiling and strong. There are black hairs on the back of his hands.

Mother The air around his stepfather seemed dark and heavy, as though he made his own weather.

The man looks up and the lad jumps, worried that he's been caught staring. But the Stepfather says nothing, takes his coat from the back of the kitchen door and goes out, banging the door behind him. The lad goes to the mirror on the wall and stares at his pale thin face.

Mother A sunny day came . . .

Boy . . . and the lad knew there was to be a trip to the travelling fair that was on in the big town. He woke early but when he came downstairs, he saw that his mother had been crying.

Pause. His stepfather walks past him without a word and goes outside to wait for his wife. The Mother cannot look her son in the eyes. She presses some coins into his palm.

Mother You're not to come to the fair. Buy yourself some lunch from the village shop. We'll be back late, so make sure you're in bed when we return.

Boy I would rather go hungry in the woods than spend your money!

He shouts and chucks the coins at his mother's feet. She shakes her head and hurries to join her husband.

Stepfather (*sneering*) Afraid of the woods though, aren't you?

The Boy leaves the coins glinting on the floor. He is seething.

Boy His stepfather was right. The lad didn't stir. Dusk came and the cottage sulked and darkened. He grew cold so he went up to bed. Hours later, the noise of his mother and stepfather returning to the cottage woke him. His door was ajar and he saw them go past on the way to their bedroom. The lamp on the landing lit up their faces, but they did not look in his room.

The days and weeks and months went on till spring, summer and autumn were gone and it was winter again.

Mother The lad moved round the house like a ghost . . .

Boy . . . and if ever he caught his mother's eye she looked away. He had stopped going to school, but nobody seemed to notice . . .

Mother One day, the lad came into the kitchen for an apple and saw his stepfather standing there.

The Boy reaches for the apple in the bowl but as he does so the Stepfather's big hand swoops down and seizes it. He looks into the man's eyes and hears the crunch as he bites into the apple.

The man strolled past him, brushing against him as though he was air, as though he was nothing.

The lad went to the mirror again, but when he gazed there he could only see the reflection of the kitchen. He leaned closer to the mirror and breathed, but the glass stayed as bright and clear as before. He pressed the flat palm of his hand against it, but although he could feel the coldness of the mirror he could see nothing of himself.

Terrified, with his heart jerking in his chest, the Boy runs upstairs to his mother's bedroom. He stares wildly into the three mirrors of the dressing table. His face is in none of them.

He fled downstairs and into the sitting room where his mother and stepfather sat.

Mother In her arms, his mother held a new baby, carefully wrapped in a soft white blanket.

Boy Mother!

Nothing.

Mother!

She is bent low over the baby's head and makes a shushing sound. The Stepfather stands up and walks towards him, tall and brooding. The lad backs away before him and the man shuts the door in his face.

And now the lad was truly invisible. He had grown in the year since his mother had married again and as no one could see him, he put on a big old shirt of his father's and went about in that. Sometimes he stood at the side of the baby's crib and looked down at his half-brother, but he was always quiet as he knew the child could not see him. At night, he lay alone on his bed, hearing his mother cry and the man shout.

Time passed.

Boy One day, finding courage in his invisibility the young man dared to walk into the forest. He was tall now and broad-shouldered. Sitting in the tree where he used to sit with his father, he saw a girl of his own age.

So used was he to being invisible, that he stood and stared at her.

The girl turned her bright hazel eyes on his and laughed at him. She reached into the foliage and tossed him an apple.

Boy He caught it low with his left hand, like a catch at cricket. It was the shiniest, reddest apple in the world. Then he remembered that he had on only his father's old shirt, which came to his knees, so he turned and ran away into the forest, clutching the apple.

But the Girl jumps down from the tree and chases him, and as she is a faster runner, she soon catches up with him. She grabs him by his shirt-tail and kisses him on the lips.

Girl Who are you?

The Boy is speechless.

I see. No voice. Let me tell you something.

A long time ago – before the invention of writing or even sign language – there was a Prince who was put under a curse by a wicked witch. He had done nothing wrong, but her evil spell was that the Prince could only speak one word each year. He was permitted to save up the words though – so that if he kept shtum for a whole year then the next year he could speak two words, and so on and so forth.

One day, he met a beautiful Princess and fell madly in love with her, body and soul. With almost superhuman effort, he set out not to speak for two whole years so that he could take her hand, look at her and say, 'My darling.' But at the end of the two years he wanted to tell her that he loved her. So he waited another three long years without uttering a peep. This brought the number of dumb years to five.

At the end of five years, he knew that he just had to ask her to marry him. So he bit his lip and endured another one, two, three, four years in total silence.

At last, as the ninth year of wordlessness ended, he took the lovely Princess to the most private and romantic spot in the royal garden and heaped a hundred red roses into her lap. Then he knelt before her, took her hand, looked into her eyes and croaked out in a hoarse voice –

'My darling! I love you! Will you marry me?'

And the Princess tidied a strand of her soft hair behind the most beautiful of ears, opened her dreamy eyes wide, parted her soft pink lips and said, 'Pardon?'

The Boy laughs hysterically and the Girl joins in. She kisses him again and runs off.

Boy When he woke the next morning, the young man climbed up to the small attic and found the chest which contained his dead father's things. He put on some soft corduroy trousers, a clean linen shirt and a beautiful leather jacket which still held the scent of wood shavings and pine. Then he pulled on warm socks and good boots.

He went downstairs to the kitchen where his mother was preparing breakfast.

Mother She stared at him and tears scalded her eyes . . .

Boy . . . and he knew that she saw him.

Girl But the girl from the woods was waiting and he went out to meet her.

Boy After a month and a day of this, he arrived home one night and found his stepfather in the kitchen.

The Stepfather looks older and smaller now that the young man has grown so tall and fit, and his black hair is greying.

Stepfather (*shouting to the Mother*) He needn't think he can come and go as he pleases.

Boy With a shock the young man realised that the man was looking at him at last.

He pushes his stepfather easily away and goes up to his bed. As he lies there in the moonlight, he hears the man's yells and his mother's wails.

The next day, the son woke early and for the first time made breakfast for his mother and her child and himself.

Stepfather As they were eating, the stepfather came in.

Boy But the son didn't glance at him and eventually the man went away.

That night, when the young man came home, he brought the girl with him so that she could meet his mother and her child.

Stepfather The stepfather came in again

Girl Just as the son was slicing up a pie, but the son ignored him until the man muttered to himself and disappeared.

Boy Every morning, the young man rose early to prepare breakfast and each night he came home with the girl and cooked supper. He worked in the forest now, chopping wood as his father had done.

Girl When the girl looked at him, she had love in her hazel eyes, like a light, and as it shone on him he grew stronger and more handsome.

Mother The mother stared at her two sons and began to notice all the ways in which they were alike. There was no more shouting or crying in the house . . .

Boy . . . and the son resolutely treated his stepfather as though he was invisible.

31

Girl The sullen man kept to himself and bothered nobody.

Mother One day he vanished altogether, taking his coat from the hook on the back of the door, and it was as though he had never been there at all.

Boy The young man worked hard in the forest to keep food on the table for the family . . .

Girl . . . and the girl took the collecting basket from the mother to gather chestnuts, hazelnuts and walnuts.

Boy They were all very happy and as his small half-brother grew, the young man made sure to watch over him, with the light of love in his eyes.

Wooden Maria

King A King and his wife had a beautiful only daughter, Maria.

Maria When Maria was fifteen, her beloved mother became fatally ill and there was nothing to be done.

King Maria's father sobbed at the Queen's side and vowed that he would never marry again.

Queen (*tenderly*) I must die. But you have our daughter to raise. I am leaving you this ring. You must promise to marry the woman whose finger fits the ring.

King The bleak mourning time passed and the King began to search for a new wife. He went from one woman to another, but the ring was too big for half of them and too small for the rest. He was secretly relieved and decided to leave things as they were for now.

Maria But one day, Maria was rummaging through her mother's things and she found the ring at the back of a drawer. She tried it on and couldn't get it off.
What will Father say?

She wraps a bandage round her finger.

King Oh dear! What have you done, Maria?

Maria Cut my finger.

King Let me see.

Maria It's nothing.

King I insist.

33

He undoes the bandage and there is the ring.

Oh my goodness, Maria! I will have to marry *you*!

Maria is shocked and laughs and cries at the same time.

Maria I can't be your wife! I'm your daughter!

King But the King was adamant he must keep to his promise.

Maria Maria went along with it on condition he bring her a dress the colour of meadows and all the flowers in the world; another dress the colour of the sea with every fish in it; and a bridal gown the colour of the sun, the moon and all the stars. She reckoned she was demanding the impossible . . .

King . . . but after six months of searching, her father presented her with the three gowns, each one in its own way the most amazing that could be imagined.

Maria One thing more.

King What else could you possibly wish for?

Maria I want another dress. Made of wood.

King The King immediately had a wooden dress made and for the first time in ages, Maria seemed pleased.

Maria On the day of the wedding, she put on the three gorgeous dresses, then the wooden dress on top, and set off for the river. She pretended to bathe then threw herself in; but instead of sinking and drowning, she floated away, down the river, out to sea, bobbing over the waves, on and on, until she came to a place where a King's son was fishing.

Prince I've never seen a fish like that.

He spreads his net and pulls her on to dry land.

Who are you and where are you from?

Maria I am Wooden Maria and I go where the water takes me.

Prince Why do you float without drowning?

Maria I am a poor girl who wears only a wooden dress that floats like a boat. Won't you let me serve you?

Prince What can you do?

Maria Everything and nothing.

Prince (*very amused*) All right. Come with me to my castle and I'll hire you as a rat-catcher, for the rats are forever plundering the eggs from the geese.

Instead of setting traps for the rats, Maria whistles and sings jolly tunes and taps out the rhythms on her wooden dress so that soon enough the rats become her pets and dance around her.

Maria She fed them on scraps from the kitchen and the rats left the geese and their eggs in peace. Every evening, Wooden Maria returned to the castle with a basket of eggs and one evening she found the King's son getting ready to go to the ball.
Where are you off to, heir to the King?

Prince Mind your own business, wooden thing!

Maria Take me dancing to the ball?

Prince You don't have a chance at all!

Maria Maria grew quiet but when she was alone she put on the dress the colour of meadows and all the flowers in the world and became the most beautiful woman ever seen.

Prince At the ball the King's son asked her at once to dance and would dance with no one else.

He fell head over heels in love with her and gave her the gold pin from his lapel.

Who are you and where are you from?

Maria I am the Countess Thwartscoff.

No one there knew her at all.

Prince Before the ball was over, she disappeared and he could not find her.

Maria She hurried home and put on her wooden dress.

Prince The following evening, the Prince dressed again for the ball.

Maria Your Highness, take me as your guest.

Prince Not in that ugly wooden dress!

Maria Take me dancing! Please be kind!

Prince Silence! I have something on my mind.

Agitated, he threatens her with a stick.

Maria After he'd gone, Maria put on the dress the colour of the sea with every fish in it. When she arrived at the ball, the guests gaped because they had never seen someone so beautiful.

Prince The men formed a queue to ask her to dance . . .

Maria . . . but she would say yes only to the King's son.

Prince Who are you and where are you from?

Maria I am the Duchess Thwartstick.

Prince Thwartstick? Is that all?

Maria The King's son was besotted and gave her the diamond ring from his pinkie. They danced and danced.

36

Prince Then suddenly she disappeared.

Maria The smitten Prince ran everywhere but no one could tell him where she had gone.

Prince The next evening as he prepared for the ball, he was in an agony of hope and despair.

Maria Your Highness . . .

As Maria approaches he shoves her roughly away.

Prince I'm in no mood for your rat-catcher's cheek.

Maria At the final ball, her beauty was dazzling, for she wore the gown the colour of the sun, the moon and all the stars.

Prince The King's son gave her the locket from round his neck which held his portrait.

He kneels enraptured at her feet and begs.

Who are you and where do you come from?

Maria Princess Thwartshove.

Prince And the next moment she had given him the slip. The King's son was struck down with love-sickness and took to his bed. Each day he grew worse, asking everyone over and over if they . . .

Maria *and* **Prince** . . . knew anything about the beautiful girl.

Prince I swear I will die unless I see her again.

Maria The whole castle thought he was bonkers. Wooden Maria heard everything and said nothing.

One day, when the King's son was more dead than alive, she slipped something in the soup the son was to sup. Not a soul saw her and the butler took him the soup.

He manages a spoonful but something sharp gets stuck in his throat and he coughs it up.

Butler You nearly swallowed a golden pin, Your Highness.

Prince (*gasping*) Thwartscoff! Who made this soup?

Butler (*worried*) The cook made it.

Prince Send for the cook! (*He scrutinises her.*) Bring me something else immediately.

Cook The cook was put out.
Tell the rat-catcher girl to fetch eggs for an omelette.

Maria But when he turned his back, she dropped the diamond ring into the mixture.

The Prince takes a bite of the omelette and nearly breaks a tooth on the diamond.

Butler You nearly broke your tooth on this diamond ring, Your Highness.

Prince Thwartstick! Who made this omelette?

Butler (*worried*) The cook made it.

Prince Summon the kitchen staff! (*He scrutinises them.*) Where did the eggs come from?

Cook Your geese, Your Highness.

Prince Tell Wooden Maria she must bake me a pie.

Cook The cook, the butler and the rest of the staff complained about this loopy behaviour . . .

Maria . . . but the pie was made and dished up soon enough.

Prince When the pining Prince forked out the locket with his portrait, he ran down to the yard.

Thwartshove! Oh, Maria, I'm sorry.

There he found the rats dancing around the girl in the wooden dress.

Rats (*singing*)
   She dresses in wood
   And loves who she should!

Maria (*singing*)
   If you live, you'll see
   This is me –
   I was born to be
   The Rat-catcher!

Prince Then Maria told him her story from beginning to end and before anyone knew it . . .

Maria . . . they were hand in glove . . .

Prince . . . and deep in love . . .

Maria . . . and wife and man . . .

Prince . . . and King and Queen . . .

Maria . . . through tears and laughter . . .

Both . . . happy ever after.

The Squire's Bride

Squire This rich Squire owned a dirty great manor and had loads of gold stashed in his chest and plenty more coming in from money-lending. But something was missing, because he was a widower. The young lass from the nearby farm worked for him and he'd taken a right shine to her. Her family was hard up and he reckoned that if he so much as hinted or winked at matrimony she'd be all over him like a rash. So he told her that he had hit upon the notion of getting wed again.

Lass (*giggling*) Ooh! It's surprising what one can hit upon!

She reckoned the revolting old goat should've hit upon something else!

Squire Well, I have hit upon the idea that *you* should be my new wife!

Lass The young girl replied prettily: thanks, but no thanks!

(*Aside.*) That day will be a long time coming, Squire! Of course, the less she wanted him . . .

Squire . . . the more he wanted her, and he wasn't used to taking no for an answer.

He got nowhere with the lass, so he sent for her father.

If the father could fix him up with the girl, he could forget about the money he owed him and the Squire would throw in that piece of land next to his field on top.

Lass The father thought his daughter was only a child who didn't know what was best for her.

Father Yes, Squire, I'll sort it, no problem.

Lass But his daughter would have none of it . . .

Father . . . whether he yelled or wheedled.

Lass I wouldn't marry the Squire if he sat in powdered gold from arsehole to earhole, so there!

Squire The Squire waited for news, day and night, but no, nowt.
   (*Angry, impatient to Father.*) I can't wait any longer. If you're to keep your promise, you must settle matters at once.

Father You're to get everything ready for the wedding and when the parson and all the guests are assembled, you're to send for the girl on a work pretext. When she arrives, she must be spliced in a trice, before she knows what's to do.

Squire (*smitten*) Good plan, good plan.

Servant So he had his servants brew and bake like maniacs . . .

Servant . . . had a wedding-cake made and a wedding punch assembled.

Squire And when everyone arrived in their finery for the feast, the Squire told one of his lads to run down to the farm and have the father send up what he'd promised. He shook his fist at the lad and told him to be back in the pop of a cork or he'd get what for.

Lad So the lad legged it.
   I've come from the Squire to fetch what you promised him. But it has to be this instant because he's in a right old state today.

Father No problem! No problem! Get down to the field and take her with you. You'll see her there.

The Lad rushes to the field and sees the Lass raking there.

Lad I'm to take what your father promised the Squire.

Lass The girl wasn't daft.
 Is that right? It's the little white mare over there by the cabbages. Take her away.

Lad The lad jumped on to the little mare's back and galloped home at full pelt.

Squire Did you get her?

Lad (*pleased*) She's standing by the front door.

Squire Well, take her up to Mother's bedroom!

Lad Bloody hell! How's that to be managed?

Squire Do as I say, and if you can't manage her on your own, get the others to help you.

Lad The Squire was puce in the face, so the lad got all the servants together . . .

Servant 1 . . . and some hauled on the front half . . .

Servant 2 . . . and some shoved on the back . . .

Lad . . . and at last they got the mare up the stairs and into the bedroom.
 I've taken her upstairs, Squire, but it was the worst job I've had since I started work here.

Squire It'll be worth it. Now send some women up to dress her.

Lad Bloody hell! How's that to be done?

Squire None of your lip! They're to get her dressed and to forget neither garter nor garland.

42

Lad Listen, girls, get yourselves upstairs and dress that little mare as a bride. The Squire must want to give his guests a good laugh.

Servant So the housemaids put the bridal outfit on the mare.

They dress her.

Lad She's ready, Squire, and wearing both garter and garland.

Squire Tickety-boo! Bring her down and I'll greet her at the door myself.

There is an almighty clattering on the stairs and the sound of snorting and neighing. The door opens, the Squire's Bride comes into the Great Hall, all the wedding guests fall about laughing.

Lass It must have been a very happy union, because they reckon the Squire hasn't gone courting since!

The Lost Happy Endings

Rat The Rat's job was important. Each evening when
dusk was removing the outlines of things, like a rubber,
the Rat had to shoulder his sack and carry all the
Happy Endings of stories from one end of the forest to
the other – in time for everybody's bedtime. Then the
Rat had to climb on to the branch of the ancient oak
tree, open the sack and shake out the Happy Endings
into the darkening air.

*Some of the Endings drift away like breath and others
flutter upwards like moths fumbling for light. Some
look like fireflies disappearing among the kindling of
the leaves and twigs and some are fireworks, zipping
skywards like rockets and flouncing off in a jackpot
of sparks high above the forest.*

When the last Ending was out of the sack, the Rat would
scamper and rustle his way homewards through the
woods. In his hole, he would sleep quite late the following
day. By the time he'd washed, eaten and visited other
rats down by the river, the Happy Endings had flown
back to the forest like homing pigeons and were hanging
from the old silver birch above his hole all ready for the
Rat to collect once more.

One evening, as the Rat set off with his sack, he
noticed scarves of mist draped in the trees. By the time
he had reached the middle of the forest, the mist had
thickened and the Rat could only see a little way ahead.

*The shadowy trees look villainous: tall ghouls with
long arms and twiggy fingers. Bushes crouch in the*

fog as though they might pounce like muggers. The eyes of owls flash like torches and make him jump; bats skim the top of his head like living frisbees and he squeaks with surprise.

Witch Hello, my verminous deario!

The Rat jumps. A twisted old Witch with a face like the bark of a tree and horrible claw hands stands on the path in front of the Rat. She has fierce red eyes like poisonous berries.

What's in the sack?

Rat Let me pass.

Witch What's in the sack, I said!

The Witch grabs hold of the Rat. Her touch nips like pepper.

Rat Let me alone! I must go on.

Witch Shut up, rodent!

She spits green spittle in the Rat's face. The Rat is so shocked that he jumps backwards and rolls over a tree root. Faster than fury, the Witch is on him and snatches the sack of Happy Endings.

I'm having this, my rat-faced deario.

She gobs at the Rat again and hobbles rapidly away into the darkness and the fog. The Rat cowers for a long time, terrified that the Witch will return.
The fog begins to lift and the moon turns the narrow path through the forest to a long silver finger. An owl's hoot questions sadly. The Rat looks about.

Rat The Happy Endings are lost!

He scatters bitter tears into the cold black night.

45

Parent As the Rat cried in the forest, children in their beds were listening to their bedtime stories. But tonight there were to be no Happy Endings.

Parent Wooden Maria sank to the bottom of the sea and she drowned.

Rat The children started to cry.

Parent The lass who worked on the farm was forced to marry the old squire and scrub him in the bath before bed.

Rat The children started to scream.

Parent The children of Hamelin, trapped inside the mountain, ate each other or starved to death.

Rat The children had hysterics.

Parent On and on the parents of the children read, and worse and worse the tales became.

Parent Soon the night was filled with the awful sound of frightened and traumatised children weeping and wailing in their beds.

A cacophony of children crying or asking for the light to be left on or refusing to sleep alone or wetting the bed. The Rat rocks back and forth moaning with sorrow.

Parent When dawn came, it grew quieter, and the exhausted Rat fell fast asleep. As he slept, he dreamed of a Golden Pen which could write on night itself.

Rat When he awoke the next morning there *was* the Golden Pen lying on the ground beside him. Without thinking, the Rat seized the pen and set off into the forest. When he came near to the spot where the witch had snitched his sack, he stopped and wondered what to do.

He holds the Golden Pen and draws a question mark on the night air. It floats before him, glowing in the darkness.

Suddenly the Rat knew exactly what to do. He would write his own Happy Ending on the night! This is what he wrote:

He writes in the air and every word shines out in perfect golden handwriting . . .

Witch When the witch first opened the sack of Happy Endings she was furious. Worthless to a witch. Boring. Stupid.

She flung the sack into the corner of her lair and went out to bite the head off any small songbird she could catch and crunch its beak. It was good to be bad. Then she decided to burn the sack of Happy Endings. She would dance around the fire and shout out terrible swear words and drink poison-berry juice and smoke a clay pipe. Good to be bad.

So she lugged the sack outside, added a few dried leaves and twigs, then squatted down and began to rub two sticks together to light the fire.

The rapid movement of her witchy hands makes a spark, then another, and another, and soon the fire is born.

Suddenly a spark leapt from the stick and jumped on to a lock of her frizzy old hair. There was a nasty burny hairy smell and – whumph!

The Witch's hair is alight. She shrieks horribly, beating at her head with her hands. She dances crazily around the fire, singing hideously. The flames dance with her, cheek to cheek, step by step, arm in arm, one-two-three, one-two-three. Her screams scatter the sleeping birds from the trees in a panic of wings.

47

Rat The Rat heard an awful noise and smelled something strange cooking. He followed his nose and it led him to the bowels of the forest. The fire opened its jaws and roared.

He stares in horror into the Witch's small red eyes until they are burned completely black and the Witch collapses in a sullen hiss of ash . . .
He sees the sack on the ground.

The sack of Happy Endings!
There was still time, if he ran as fast as he ever had in his life, to send the Happy Endings out into the world . . .

Parent . . . goosegirls went to the ball and grooms lived happily ever after . . .

Parent Squires with little taste and loads of cash produced as much food as a peasant could ever wish for and . . .

Rat Look! Look! Look! Lost children are running home through the woods into the arms of their parents.

They celebrate.

The End.

RATS' TALES

the stories by
CAROL ANN DUFFY

Rats and the Chinese Zodiac

Rats!

Members of the genus *rattus* – black or brown –
Found in countryside and town.
Long-tailed rodents, live in packs;
Collective noun, *mischief* of Rats.
Blamed for the fleas upon their backs
Who brought the plague in the Middle Ages
On the ships that sailed to here from Asia.
Unfair!

Rats!

Expert jumpers, climbers, swimmers.
Love their food – they're no slimmers!
The second most successful mammal
On the planet? Fact – the Rat!
They go where you go – gnawing, chewing.
No Rat is ever more than ten feet from a human.

Rats!

Colour-blind. Fantastic sense of smell.
From their whiskers they can tell
Exactly where they are – how far, how near.
They can disappear down a sewer, down a well.
Rats are clever, sociable, untemperamental.
In India, they have their very own and sacred Hindu
  temple!

Rats!

Who can say why cats chase Rats?

It's all to do with the Chinese Zodiac.

A long, long time ago when the world was still young, all the creatures on the planet were good friends and true comrades. Everyone liked everyone else and there was never any trouble. In fact, although you might find this hard to believe, the Cat and the Rat were so close and were such terrific pals that they shared a house. One day, it was announced that all the animals in China were invited to enter a competition to win a place in the twelve signs of the Zodiac. There was going to be a long and hard race and the winner would become the first sign of the Zodiac; the second would become the second sign of the Zodiac; the third would become the third sign of the Zodiac; the fourth would . . . Well, it's quite obvious how matters were to be arranged. The animals were incredibly excited about this wonderful opportunity, but the Cat and the Rat were anxious. The thing was, they were both addicted to sleeping, snoozing and snoring, and they were very worried that they would miss the start of the big race. The Cat and the Rat discussed this mutual problem at considerable length before deciding to ask their friend, the Ox, to make quite sure that they woke up in good time for the off. The loyal Ox agreed and gave his solemn word.

So – the day of the great race dawned and the Ox made his way to the home of the Cat and the Rat while the dew was still wet on the cherry blossom. *Bang! Bang! Bang!* he went on the front door with his great big mighty hoof – but there was no reply! *Bellow! Bellow! Bellow!* he roared at the window with his great big mighty voice – but there was no reply! So the Ox broke down the door with his great big mighty shoulder and barged into the bedroom to meet the Cat and the Rat as he had promised.

Would you credit it? The two bone-idle specimens were so deeply asleep in their stinking pit that nothing the Ox did could wake them up (and he tried *everything*!) The Ox saw that it was getting late, so he picked up the Cat and the Rat, put them on his great big mighty back, and made his way to the start of the race. *On your marks! Get set! Go!*

The race began and the Ox ran as fast as he could, still with the Cat and the Rat in the land of Nod on his broad back. If the Ox could *win* the race, then all three of the gang would be part of the Zodiac! Of course, all the bouncing up and down on top of the Ox at last woke up the Rat!

He looked across and there was the Cat, still kipping away, and the Rat suddenly had a brainwave! If the Cat were to wake up and start running, there was totally no way the Rat could beat her. The Cat was so much bigger and faster than the Rat. So he gave the Cat a good shove and she fell straight off the back of the Ox! The poor Cat bounced twice on the ground, rolled into the ice-cold river and was at once wide awake! She splashed and crawled her way out of the water just in time to see all the other animals racing past her and speeding away. The Ox was almost at the finishing line when the Rat climbed up on to his head – and just before the Ox broke the tape to win the race, the Rat jumped forwards as far as he possibly could and managed to beat the Ox by a whisker!

This is why the Rat is the first sign of the Chinese Zodiac (and the Ox is the second). But as for the Cat, she never forgave the Rat for pushing her off the Ox's back and into the river. To this very day, instead of being good friends, true comrades and sharing a home, Cats chase Rats as soon as they see them. Like this!

The Pied Piper of Hamelin

A long time ago in the town of Hamelin, which is still there, there was an invasion of rats the like of which it is impossible for us to imagine, but we will try. These rats were dirty great black things which ran as they pleased in broad daylight through the streets and swarmed all over the houses so that folk couldn't put their hand or foot down without touching something furry. When dressing in the morning they found rats in their underpants and petticoats, in their hats, boots, briefcases and pockets. One poor citizen had found two rats playing in her brassiere.

When anyone wanted a bite to eat, the rats had been there first! The Cook, for example, was always going into her larder and finding that the rats had eaten the cheese or sucked the eggs or nibbled the bread or gnawed the rind off the best bacon. The Cook had a good moan about it to the Priest, who agreed with her, because he had found rats in the pockets of his cassock, and had had his King James Bible chewed from Genesis to Revelations. In fact, there was nowt left of his Holy Candle but the wick!

The Priest had a right old bitch about it with the Poet, who agreed with him because she couldn't write poetry any more on account of the noise. As soon as it got dark, the rats set to work, nibbling away from cellar to garret. Everywhere, in the ceilings, in the floors, in the cupboards, at the doors, there was a scamper and a rummage, and such a furious noise of gimlets, pincers and saws, that the Poet was a nervous wreck! So the townsfolk agreed to march to the Town Hall and find the Politician to demand that something was done about the bloody rats.

The Politician announced that they were all in this

together and he would launch an Official Inquiry . . . but at this everyone plonked themselves down on their bottoms and refused to budge until the Politician came up with a better idea.

Well, they sat there from noon till dusk while the Politician consulted his Moral Compass and looked at his Legacy and mentioned his Mandate, when there arrived in the town a man with an unusual face, who played on a pipe and sang these words:

> 'If you live, you'll see
> This is me –
> I was born to be
> The Rat-catcher!'

He was an odd, gawky person, very weatherbeaten, with a long crooked nose, a droopy rat-tail moustache, and two great yellow piercing eyes under a felt hat with a crimson feather. He was dressed in a green jacket, red pantaloons and big leather boots. He stopped outside the Town Hall, with his back to the Church, and continued with his music, singing:

> 'If you live, you'll see
> This is me –
> I was born to be
> The Rat-catcher!'

The Politician came rushing from the Town Hall, followed by the citizens, and the Pied Piper explained that if they made it worth his while, he would get rid of all their rats, right down to the last one.

'He's not from round here!' cried the citizens with one voice. 'He might trick us! We can't trust him!'

But the Politician knew a potential vote-winner when he saw one! He was determined that it was high time everyone went home and stopped blaming him for the rats. So he said, 'I give you my word of honour, Piper, that you will be properly rewarded, should you succeed in ridding our town of rats. How much do you charge?'

'By midnight tonight, I shall remove every rat from this place, if you promise to pay me one gold sovereign for each rat.'

'One gold sovereign for each rat!' cried the citizens with one voice. But that will come to millions of pounds!'

But despite the grumbling of the people, the Politician was not for turning. He shook hands with the Piper, gave him a beaming smile, and guaranteed to pay him one gold sovereign for every rat with the taxpayers' own money.

The Piper replied that he would start this evening when the moon rose. He requested that the inhabitants leave the streets empty, but said that they could look out of their windows at what was happening and that it would be an interesting event. And so, at about nine o'clock that night, the Pied Piper reappeared by the Town Hall, back to the Church, and as the moon rose on the horizon, he began to play on his pipe.

At first the music was slow and dreamy, gentle as a caress; but then it grew more and more lively as though it was saying, 'Come and dance!' It could be heard loud and clear in the farthest alley of the town. Soon, from the depths of the cellars and sewers, from the tops of the attics and garrets, from out of the larders, cupboards, wardrobes, handbags and wellingtons, from under the beds and tables, from every corner of every house or shop . . . out came the rats! They ran out of the doors, jumped into the street and tap, tap, tap, began to dance, all squeezed together, towards the Town Hall. There were so many of them they looked like a filthy flood in full flow.

When the square was completely rammed, the Piper turned away and, still playing wonderfully, magically, began to walk towards the river at the foot of the town. The rats followed eagerly until the Piper stopped playing and pointed to the middle of the river where the water was flowing and swirling and foaming and whirling dangerously.

'Hop! Hop!' he cried. 'Hop! Hop!' And straight away, without pausing for a moment, the rats began to jump in, head first, one after another, and disappeared. It was almost midnight when, at the very end of the line, crawling along slowly, came a big old rat, silver with age. It was the boss of the plague.

'Are they all in, my old friend?' asked the Piper.

'They are all in, brother,' replied the silver rat.

'And how many were there?'

'Nine hundred and ninety thousand, nine hundred and ninety-nine.'

'Including you?'

'Including me!'

'Then go and join them, old friend, till we meet again.'

Then the silver rat jumped into the river and disappeared.

The Piper had kept his end of the bargain and went off to his bed at the inn. And for the first time in a long, long while, the citizens of Hamelin slept peacefully through the night and the Poet was able to start at last on a new poem.

The next morning, just after nine o'clock, the Pied Piper arrived outside the Town Hall, where all the well-rested and breakfasted citizens had already gathered and were cheering and applauding the Politician.

'All your rats went for a swim in the river last night,' called out the Piper, 'and I guarantee not one will return. There were nine hundred and ninety thousand, nine hundred and ninety-nine, at one gold sovereign a head. It is time to count out my wages.

'Just a moment, stranger,' smiled the Politician. One sovereign a head means one head a sovereign. Where are the heads?'

The taxpayers roared with laughter, but the Piper had

not expected this devious ploy. He shook with rage and his eyes burned red.

'The heads?' he hissed. 'If you want the heads, then go and find them in the river!'

'Oh, I see!' boomed the Politician confidently. 'You are refusing to keep to the terms of our arrangement. One sovereign per head. Where are the heads?'

The crowd joined in with one voice: 'Where are the heads? Where are the heads? Show us the heads!'

'Order! Order!' cried the Politician, in charge once more. He turned to the Piper and said, 'We could refuse even to pay you a penny. But we are a Big Society and you have been of use to us. Why not accept a token ten sovereigns for your trouble, before you leave?'

'Keep your token ten sovereigns,' replied the Piper poisonously. 'If you do not pay me, I will be paid by your children.'

Then he pulled his hat down over his eyes, turned away, and left the town without speaking to a soul.

The taxpayers gave high-fives and slapped each other on the back and laughed when the Politician said the Rat-catcher had been caught in his own trap. But what made them laugh most of all was his threat of passing their debt on to their children.

The next day was a Sunday and they all went happily to the Church, looking forward to a Sunday lunch after Mass that hadn't been sampled by rats.

But when everyone returned home to his or her house, their children had gone.

'Our children! Where are our children?' was the terrible cry that was heard in every street.

Then, limping from the east side of the town, came a little lame boy who was sobbing loudly and this is what he told,

While all the adults were at Church, a wonderful music had started. Soon, all the boys and girls who had been left safely at home had run outside, following the magical sound to the square by the Town Hall. They found the Pied Piper there, playing his music just as he had on the night he caught all the rats. Then the Piper had walked quickly towards the east gate of the town and all the children had followed, running, singing, clapping, dancing to the music, as far as the foot of the mountain outside Hamelin. But when they got near, the mountain had opened and the Piper had gone in, still playing his music, and all the children had danced after him, after which the mountain had closed again. The only child left was the lame boy who could not keep up with the others.

When they heard this story, the parents wailed in horror and distress. They ran with sledgehammers and pikes to the mountain, and banged at the rock till darkness, searching for the opening. The Politician, who had lost three little boys and two little girls, clawed at the stone with his bare hands, but it was all useless. When night fell, the citizens had to return to Hamelin without their children, and only the cold face of the moon was witness to the dreadful sights and sounds of their grief.

The Stolen Childhood

A stepmother lived with her dead husband's young daughter. The girl was sweet-natured and lovely, but the stepmother had a heart that had soured and shrivelled under her black frock. Her hair had dried and rusted on her head and she took pleasure in nothing.

Day after day, she watched her stepdaughter as she played in the garden and the stepmother's blood clogged with envy as she saw the young girl chasing butterflies or turning cartwheels or singing to herself in the arms of the apple tree. More than anything, the stepmother yearned and burned to be young again.

One day, a stranger came to the town and took a room at the inn. The stepmother, staring as usual from her window, noticed the stranger walking in the lane. He was tall and dark and as the woman gazed down at him, he glanced up and spied her. With one look he saw into her dark soul and knew what she wanted.

'Come to me,' he said, and she heard him and jumped, as though a poker were stirring the burnt coals and ashes of her heart. She hurried outside into the lane to stand beside him.

Close up she could see that there was no kindness in his face and she shivered. He was holding a pair of sharp silver scissors.

'I can give you what you most want,' he said. 'Take these scissors and cut the shadow from the first young person you find asleep. Then you must snip off your own shadow and throw it over the young person without waking them. Their youth will be yours at once and they will be as old as you are now.'

'What must I pay you for this?' asked the stepmother, because she knew very well there would be a price.

'You will be my bride,' he answered, 'on the happiest day of your life.'

The stepmother gave a dry laugh and thought that the man was joking, but she agreed to his strange bargain and took the scissors. He walked rapidly away down the lane and quite soon after that he left the town.

The stepmother went into the garden holding the scissors, which glittered in her hand in the sunlight.

Her young stepdaughter was stretched out on the lawn with her straw hat over her face, fast asleep in the warm buttery sun. Her shadow lay on the grass beside her, so cool and dark that already the daisies there had started to close.

The stepmother knelt down, silent as poison, and cut along the whole length of the girl's shadow. A breeze blew under it and lifted it gently, but the stepmother snatched at it, crumpling it up and stuffing it in her skirt pocket. It felt like the softest silk.

Then the stepmother stood and saw her own long shadow at her feet. She bent down and with a *snap!* and a *snip!* she cut it off. She lifted her heavy, leathery shadow and tossed it over the sleeping girl, then turned and ran towards the house to look in the mirror. Her step felt lighter and for the first time in years she noticed all the different smells of the garden as she ran.

The stepdaughter felt something heavy and sour-smelling upon her and opened her eyes in fright. It was dark. She screamed and tried to jump up but her body felt stiff and strange and her back ached.

She sat up and pushed the shadow away from her and it lay in a heap like an old black coat.

'How horrible!' cried the girl.

She touched her throat. Her voice was different, deeper and harsher, not like a child's voice at all. She looked at her hands. They were like a pair of crumpled gloves, several sizes too big, the skin loose and creased over the bones.

She stood up slowly, holding the small of her back, and heard the waxy creak of her knees. Truly scared now, she hurried as fast as she could, a bit out of breath, to look in the mirror.

The mirror was a full-length one and hung in the shadowy hall. The stepmother was standing before it and she turned her head as she heard the sound of her stepdaughter behind her. Both of them stared at each other in disbelief and then the stepmother began to laugh, the light easy laugh of a young girl.

'Look at yourself!' she cried and pulled her stepdaughter to the mirror.

A middle-aged face stared back from the glass, grey-haired and lined. The stepdaughter's teeth felt strange and uncomfortable in her mouth and when she touched them with her tongue she realised that they were false. She began to cough and the bitter taste of tobacco scalded the back of her throat. She turned to her stepmother.

Her stepmother was smaller, with soft hair the colour of a conker and skin as delicate as the petal of a rose. She was jumping up and down and clapping her hands.

'It worked! It worked!' she cried. 'I am young again and *you* have all my years!'

Then the stepmother spun round and ran back into the sunshine and the poor stepdaughter fell to the floor in the dark hall and sobbed bitterly.

Summer turned, as it has to do, into autumn and autumn soon became winter.

It was the stepdaughter now who stood at the window, a shawl round her cold stiff bones, watching the village children throw snowballs in the field on the other side of the lane.

She wondered why her young stepmother never played with the others, why she never helped to make a snowman

– pushing a snowball along till it doubled and trebled and quadrupled in size, creaking under her mittens. And why she never hopped and whistled her way to school with the other children or pressed her nose to the toyshop window or scraped a stick along the green railings of the park. What was the point of her stepmother being young at all?

A fierce headache tightened round her brow, deepening the frowns and creases on her papery skin, and she turned away from the window and went to lie down on the bed in her hushed, dull room. She was always tired now.

She took out her teeth and put them in a glass of water on the bedside table. They grinned away at her as though Death himself had come to call.

But downstairs the stepmother pulled on her boots and went for a walk in the snow, ignoring the shouts of the children playing in the field.

'Youth,' she sneered to herself, 'is wasted on the young.'

She walked for miles, breathing in the clean cold air and not feeling the faintest bit tired, working up a good hunger for dinner.

She grabbed a fistful of snow and sucked at it, gasping at the cold. She was young again! Young! Her skin and her eyes and her hair sparkled in the hard white winter light.

Winter turned to spring then summer then autumn then winter then spring then summer . . .

The stepmother was taller now and beautiful and many young men came to the house to visit her. They brought flowers and perfume and chocolates and told her that they adored her, and that she was the loveliest young girl in the village, that her lips were rubies and her eyes were sapphires and that each little nail on the tips of her fingers was a pearl.

'I am in the springtime of my life,' gloated the stepmother. 'Again!'

Her stepdaughter watched the young men come and go from her window, but none of them so much as glanced up at the sad old woman with the dull eyes and the yellowing teeth.

One young man, the stepdaughter thought, was handsomer and jollier than all the rest, and her heart, tired as it was, would skip a beat as though it had almost remembered something, whenever she saw him.

At night she would dream that she was dancing and laughing in his arms, a girl once more. But when she woke up she was alone, brittle and aching in the mothbally shroud of her nightgown.

As the summer passed, she noticed that the young man came more and more often to the house to visit her stepmother and that the other boys had drifted way.

On the first day of autumn her stepmother and the young man came before her and told her that they were to be married. Her tired heart sank like a stone in her chest as she looked at the young man and she knew then that she loved him, but she kissed her stepmother and wished her happiness.

'Oh, I will be happy,' answered the stepmother. 'My wedding day will be the happiest day of my life.'

The stepmother had decided to be married at Christmas. The days fell from the calendar like leaves from the trees and, quicker than the snip of scissors, it was the morning of Christmas Eve.

The wedding was to be at noon and already the bell-ringers were swinging from their ropes, sending the warm bronze voices of the bells across the frozen fields. The bride was to be driven from the house to the church in a white carriage pulled by a chestnut horse. The stepdaughter was to ride behind her in a plain wooden carriage.

As the bells chimed eleven o'clock, the stepdaughter was standing in the lane waiting for the carriages to arrive. The cold bit through her dark winter coat into her bones.

'Here I am!' Her stepmother stood at the door of the house in a dress of silver and gold. 'How do I look?'

'You look good enough to eat,' said a harsh voice from the lane.

The stepdaughter saw the shock and surprise on her stepmother's face and turned to see who had spoken.

A tall man with a mean face and fierce eyes had appeared from nowhere and stood staring intensely at the bride. 'Our carriage will soon be here.'

'Our carriage?' said the stepmother. 'You must be mistaken!'

All the colour had drained from her face until she was paler than the late white roses that she carried in her hands.

'Come,' said the stranger impatiently. 'You know very well what is to happen today.'

'Today is to be the happiest day of my life,' replied the stepmother in a trembling voice. 'I am to marry the young man who loves me.'

'You are to marry me, my beauty,' said the tall man, 'and you can forget about love. Come!'

'Marry you?' said the bride. 'You?' She laughed hysterically.

The sound of horses' hooves clattered suddenly in the lane and the stepmother ran to her stepdaughter and clutched at her arm. She had started to cry and the stepdaughter could see that she was shaking with fear.

'Who is he?' she asked the terrified bride.

The carriages had arrived, but one was a closed ebony carriage drawn by four black horses who steamed and snorted in the lane.

'Get into the carriage!' said the stranger as he flung open the door.

'No! No! You can't make me!' The stepmother was sobbing now and quite wild with terror and the stepdaughter felt real dread, colder than ice, chilling her heart.

'Who is he? Tell me!' she said again.

'For the last time,' said the man, 'get into the carriage.'

But the stepmother looked into his eyes and saw all the

badness of this world and the next and would not go. She shook her head.

The stranger gave a twisted smile and stared hard at the bride.

'You have broken your promise,' he said. 'Put your hand in the pocket of your dress.'

The stepmother did as she was told and pulled out a small piece of crumpled black silk. She gave a little scream and dropped it, and it floated down to the ground and landed at her stepdaughter's feet.

Then the tall man pulled off his coat and the step-daughter saw that it was the old black coat that had nearly suffocated her when she was a child. With a quick movement the stranger threw it over her stepmother, completely covering her lovely gold and silver dress.

'Don't!' she screamed. 'I'll come! I'll come!'

'Too late,' said the man, and he climbed into the ebony carriage. The four black horses tossed their heads and neighed and began to move away.

'Come back!' screeched the stepmother, but the carriage gathered speed, reached the bend at the top of the lane and vanished. The clatter of hooves faded into the distance.

The stepmother flung away the coat and turned to face her stepdaughter. 'Help me!' she said. 'What am I to do?'

Her stepdaughter was staring at her in horror. The stepmother's beautiful dress hung in tattered grey rags from her bony shoulders. Her hair had turned white and clumps of it had fallen from her head, leaving some of it bald. Her mouth had shrunk inwards in a small wrinkled O of disappointment, as though her lips were mourning her vanished teeth. Her body shrivelled and stooped till she looked like a question mark asking, *Why? Why? Why?*

She was five times as old as before and her voice when she spoke was the dusty croak of a crone. 'Why do you stare at me?'

Then she clutched at her throat and gaped at her step-daughter. Colour had flooded back into the stepdaughter's hair, a glowing red-blonde, and the girl was smiling at her with perfect white teeth.

'What is happening to me?' she said, and when she heard the light music of her own voice she laughed with delight. 'Stepmother! I am myself again!'

She felt her young lungs breathing easily and her heart opened like a flower in her breast.

There were running footsteps in the lane and it was the bridegroom, out of breath and looking for the bride. He glanced curiously at the old witch, bent double by the ditch, coughing and cursing, but as soon as he saw the girl he had eyes only for her.

'Your bride has gone,' she said to him.

'I am sorry to hear that,' he said politely, but his eyes burned with sudden love as he looked at her.

There was a strange noise from the ditch and they both turned to see the old black coat lying in a heap on the road. There was no sign of the stepmother, but a sudden gust of wind blew a handful of ashes, grey and gritty, over the fields.

'Your bride has gone for ever,' repeated the girl.

'My bride was lovely,' said the young man, 'but you are truly the most beautiful girl I have ever seen in my life.'

The girl looked down at her hands and saw the light of youth that glowed under her skin and she felt the force and energy of life itself rise up from the tingling tips of her toes so that all she wanted to do was run!

'Catch me if you can!' She laughed at the young man and took to her heels, flinging off her heavy winter coat as she went.

With a shout, laughing himself, he chased her, never quite catching her, his pounding feet landing on her slim fast shadow as she ran before him.

A Little Girl

A Little Girl lived with her little family in a Doll's House.

There was Little Grandma, who had her own room at the top of the house.

There was Little Grandad, who dozed in a rocking chair in front of the fire all day, even in summer.

There was Little Mother, who spent most of her time in the kitchen, cooking.

And there was Little Twin, the Little Girl's twin sister, who shared her bedroom and slept above the Little Girl in the top bunk.

Every morning, the little family would eat breakfast together in the kitchen and Little Mother would serve tiny boiled eggs in teeny egg cups and the weeniest glasses of orange juice.

After breakfast, Little Grandma would climb up the stairs to her room, sit on a little chair and stare out of the window.

Little Grandad rocked himself slowly to sleep in front of the orange and crimson fire while Little Mother tidied away the breakfast things; and the Little Girl and her Little Twin went to the drawing room to play on the little upright piano or read wee books or dance together. The afternoons ticked away, the two children throwing a red ball between them, the size of a berry. Every day was the same and, whenever the Little Girl asked to go outside, her mother shushed her or her grandparents tutted or her sister shook her head.

At night, when the house grew dark, tiny lamps came on in the Doll's House and the little family sat together round the fire until it was time for bed. Then the Little

Girl lay in her bottom bunk with her eyes wide open, listening to the thick deep silence of the darkness.

One morning, the Little Girl looked across at her Little Twin and noticed that she seemed smaller. The Little Girl thought that perhaps she was imagining this, but her own tiny black shoes no longer fitted and she had to go about the house barefooted since they were her only pair.

When she sat down for breakfast, she found that her chair was too small for her and her knees scraped on the underside of the kitchen table. She was still hungry after she'd eaten her boiled egg and toast and still thirsty after she'd drained her weeny glass of orange juice, but nobody else seemed to notice these things, so the Little Girl said nothing.

Later, when she asked whether she might go outside, her mother shushed her and her grandparents tutted and her sister shook her head. That night, as she lay in her bunk, her feet poked out from under her blankets and her head pressed hard against the wall behind her pillow, so she gathered her bedclothes together and stretched out on the floor till morning came.

When the light from outside arrived, she sat up to discover that her head was at the same height as her Little Twin's bunk bed.

Little Twin started to cry as she looked at her sister's large, pale face, a breathing moon, then she ran downstairs to the kitchen, calling for Little Mother.

From then on, the Little Girl grew apart from the rest of her family. They looked at her strangely as she squeezed herself through the little doors of the Doll's House or stooped and knelt to avoid banging her head on the ceilings.

They complained bitterly when they found that she had eaten the entire contents of their little fridge to satisfy her hunger. They whispered to themselves when she knocked over the furniture as she passed.

Curled in the attic, the largest space in the house, the Little Girl heard the fierce squeaks of her family's voices far below. She lifted her arms above her head, carefully raised the red-tiled roof of the Doll's House and climbed outside.

Now that she could stand at her full height, the Little Girl saw that she was as tall as the Doll's House. The chimneys looked like boxes of matches; the front door like a cigarette packet. The windows seemed no bigger than playing cards. She put her eye to the glass of her grandmother's room. Little Grandma sat in her chair staring out through her window, still and unblinking. She looked, the Little Girl thought, just like a wax doll.

She knelt down and peered in through the drawing-room window. Little Grandad was asleep in his rocking chair in front of the orange and crimson fire which never burned down.

Her sister, Little Twin, was reading the same page of a wee book over and over again.

The Little Girl's eyes filled with tears which fell and splashed against the window like rain.

She stretched out and leaned on her elbow to peep through the kitchen window where Little Mother stood at the table ready to tidy away the breakfast things. More than anything, the Little Girl wished that for once her mother would put on the teeny hat and weeny coat that hung from the hook on the kitchen door, walk out of the kitchen, along the hall and out through the front door.

All day, she stared and peeped and squinted through the windows of the Doll's House, noticing the bath the size of a soap dish, the piano the size of a mouth organ, the fridge the size of a choc ice. That night, the Little Girl lay down on the floor outside the Doll's House. She could see the tiny lights go out inside the house as she drifted away into sleep.

When she awoke, she was even bigger than before. There was a big comfy-looking bed with plump pillows in the room she was in, a large wooden wardrobe full of clothes which fitted her perfectly and several pairs of shoes that were just the right size for her feet. She chose a lovely red dress and a pink pair of soft leather boots.

Delicious cooking smells were coming from below. Her Tall Mother smiled at her as she entered the kitchen and said that they'd be having breakfast in the garden. The kitchen window was open and the whole wide wonderful world stretched endlessly away in the morning sunlight.

So the girl grew and grew and the Doll's House stayed in the corner of her bedroom. She peeped in through its windows at first, but soon she forgot to do this, for she had her own big windows now and she could see the stars.

She went outside whenever she wished and travelled far and wide under the sun and under the moon. In time, she went to live in another house and the Doll's House was packed away and forgotten. She became a woman and had her own family and, though she had her troubles from time to time as everyone does, she was very happy for many years.

One day, the woman looked in the mirror and saw that she had become old. There were silver threads in her hair and fine lines on her face. Her own daughter had grown now and had long since moved away and her son was a man who lived in a distant country.

One day, she went up to the attic to store some apples that needed ripening and saw, tucked away in a corner, the old Doll's House.

She knelt before it and peered in through one of the upstairs windows. Little Grandma was sitting in her chair, staring sightlessly out. The woman's heart gave a horrible lurch and her breath came out in a gasp, covering the window with a fine mist. She rubbed at the glass with a corner of her sleeve and Little Grandma stared right through her just as before.

Then the old woman looked into the window of her old bedroom and saw that both the little bunk beds were empty, so she crouched lower and peeped into the drawing-room window.

Little Twin sat quietly, reading a wee book, and Little Grandad was asleep in the rocking chair in front of the orange and crimson fire.

The woman tapped on the pane with her fingernail but Little Twin didn't look up from her wee book and Little Grandad slept on.

The woman felt herself shrinking with longing and regret.

She moved her head till it was level with the kitchen window. Little Mother stood at the table as she always had. The woman's heart brimmed with love, like a glass filling with the finest wine, and without thinking she banged hard on the glass with her fists.

Then Little Mother was waving and smiling at her and had run down the hall to fling open the front door and she felt her Little Twin's tiny hand in hers, pulling her inside, and heard the small excited clucks of Little Grandma and Little Grandad as they walked towards her. The door closed behind her with a small click.

That night the Little Girl stood at her bedroom window as her little family slept. Outside the Doll's House, planets glowed and shone like giant apples far out in the endless universe.

The Maiden with No Hands

A King once became a widower and had no wife by his side. He fretted and sulked about this until the Devil put it into his head that he should marry his own sister. Her name was Penta. The selfish, spoilt King sent for Penta one day and said, 'Sister, a man of good judgement never allows anything valuable to leave his house. Plus, you never know what might occur if a stranger were to show up. I know you very well, your character and so on, and I value you, of course, so I have decided you shall be my next wife and must settle down to the business of being a useful partner to me. There! Just what the doctor ordered.'

When Penta heard these outrageous words she was shocked to the core and thought her brother must be mad. She went red in the face and exclaimed, 'Are you out of your tiny mind? I can't believe what you've just suggested. If it's meant to be funny, it's foolhardy! If it's meant to be serious, it's stupid! If it's meant to be practical, it's pathetic! We are brother and sister, you cuckoo! Pay attention! If my virtuous ears ever hear such words again from your slimy tongue, I'll do something to surprise you! If you do not treat me like a sister, then I shall not treat you as a brother!'

Penta fled to her room, locked and bolted the door behind her, and did not see her brother for a whole month. The wretched King was left to skulk around as though his face had been walloped by a sledgehammer. He was as furtive as a boy who has smashed a window and as confused as a cook who has seen the dog run off with the sausages. Nevertheless, when Penta eventually appeared, he was at it again, trying to persuade her to go into partnership as a wife because he was a lonely widower.

'No, no, no, no, no,' said Penta. 'I'm your sister! What is it about me that could possibly make you think I could be your wife?'

'Penta,' replied the King, 'it is your hands! Like forks they draw out the core of my heart from my chest. Like hooks they lift the bucket of my soul from the well of my being. Like pincers they grip my spirit tightly while love smooths it like a file. Oh, hands! Beautiful hands! They are ladles spooning out sweetness! They are pliers extracting promises! They are shovels digging in my consciousness!'

Hearing this claptrap, Penta told him to be quiet, even though he wanted to say more. 'I've heard enough,' she said. 'Stay there and don't go away. I'll be right back.'

She went to her room, called a servant who was as daft as a banana, gave him a knife and some gold, and said to him, 'Boy, cut my hands off. I want to give them a special manicure.'

The servant thought he was doing her a favour and cut her hands off – *chop! chop!* – with two clean blows. Penta had them put in a bowl and covered with a cloth, then sent to her brother with a message telling him to enjoy the hands that he admired so much and wishing him a good life. The King was livid. He had a trunk built and smeared with tar. Then he ordered his sister to be pushed inside and thrown into the sea.

The trunk was tossed about by the waves, then landed on a beach where some fishermen sorting their nets discovered it. They were amazed to find the beautiful Penta inside. One of the men was also the chief of the island and he took her home and told his wife to be kind to her. But the fishwife was jealous of Penta's beauty and bundled her back into the trunk and launched it into the sea.

The trunk was swallowed up by the waves and battered about back and forth until it was spotted by a ship in which a foreign King was sailing. He had a boat lowered into the water to fetch the trunk and bring it on board. When it was opened and the kind King saw such a living beauty in that coffin of death he swore he had found great treasure, even if it was a casket of jewels without handles. He took Penta to his kingdom and gave her as a lady-in-waiting to the Queen. Penta served her as well as she could with her feet, even cooking for her, threading needles, ironing her dresses, and combing her hair. The Queen grew as fond of Penta as though she were her own daughter.

But sadly, after a while the Queen grew ill and knew she had to die. She was resigned to this and told her husband that if he loved her and wanted her to be happy in death, he must promise her to marry Penta after the Queen closed her eyes and turned to dust.

The King said, 'I hope you live another hundred years, my darling. However if you must go to that other world and leave me in darkness, I swear to you that I will take Penta for my wife. I don't care that she has no hands so long as I give you a sign of how much I love you in death.' And after the Queen had extinguished the candle of her days, he kept his promise and Penta was soon expecting a child.

The King had to undertake another journey by sea and he said goodbye to Penta and set sail. Nine months later, Penta gave birth to a dazzling boy and the whole kingdom was lit up. The King's advisers sent him a letter bearing this wonderful news, but the ship carrying the letter was caught up in a storm and washed up on the beach where the fishermen had first found Penta in the trunk. The wife who had betrayed Penta was walking there and asked the ship's captain where he was headed. The captain told her everything about the King marrying Penta the Handless and that he must deliver a letter containing great news concerning Penta to the King. Hearing this, the treacherous fishwife invited the captain for a drink and deliberately set out to get him drunk. As soon as he passed out, she found the letter in his pocket. When she read about the baby, she was consumed with envy. She forged another letter saying that Penta had given birth to a little dog, and that the King's advisers were awaiting the King's orders. She swapped the letters and put the false one back in the captain's pocket.

When he awoke – with an awful hangover – and saw the weather had improved, he set sail again to deliver the letter to the King. The King replied at once, instructing his advisers to cheer up the Queen and tell her that these things happened. She was not to have a moment's regret because such matters were ordained by heaven and no human being could influence the stars!

He sent the captain on his way and the gullible captain decided to drop anchor at the beach and visit the fishwife for another drink. Once more she filled him with booze so that he passed out. She read the King's letter and replaced it with a false one which ordered the royal advisers to burn the mother and son as soon as they read it.

But when the forgery reached them, the King's advisers, those wise old men, discussed it for a long time, murmuring and pondering. They concluded that the King was either crazy or bewitched, because he had a pearl of a wife and a diamond of a son and could not possibly be allowed to drop such jewels into the empty hand of death. It seemed better to them to choose a middle way, so they gave the Queen a handful of coins to support herself and her child and sent them away never to return.

Poor Penta took her son in her stunted arms and set off, weeping and wandering. She arrived in a place which was ruled by a magician. When he saw the beautiful maimed maiden who maimed everyone's heart, he wanted to hear the whole story of her misfortunes, right from the beginning when her brother had so appallingly mistreated her. After he had heard everything, the magician could not stop crying. But he gave her a spendid set of rooms in his palace and ordered that she was to be treated as his daughter. Then he issued a proclamation that whoever came to his court and told the most impressive tale of great misfortune would receive a golden crown and sceptre that were worth more than the whole country!

Well, of course, once the proclamation began to spread, more people than there were beetles and caterpillars began to arrive at the magician's palace. One man told how he had worked all his life at a court and had been given only a lump of cheese for his pension. Another man had been kicked in the arse every day for five years by his employer and could do nothing about it. There was a chap who sobbed aloud as he told how his wife was allergic to him and sneezed without stopping if he came near her, so they had no children. Then there was a woman whose nose was so long that dogs chased after her in the street, barking with delight.

Meanwhile, the King had returned home and discovered that everything was heartbreak and bitterness. He was about to have his advisers flogged and skinned when they showed him the letter. When he saw that it was forged, he sent for the captain and heard all about the fisherman's wife on the beach. Realising that she had done all this, he set sail at once and found her himself.

This time, the wife was plied with fine wine by the King and he got the whole story from her, beginning to end. When he learned what she had done to Penta, simply out of jealousy, he ordered that she be made into a candle. So she was waxed and greased and stuck on top of a huge pile of dry wood. The King himself lit the match and when he saw her dance a horrible tango with the hot red fire, he got up and sailed away.

Out on the high seas, he passed another ship carrying the King who was Penta's brother, who told him about the magician's proclamation. The weak brother reckoned that nobody in the world had suffered the misery and bad luck that he had, and was on his way to try for the reward.

'If that's the way of it,' said the King, 'I can beat you with my hands tied behind my back. In fact, I can beat anyone, my agony and misfortune have been so relentlessly awful. Let's agree to compete like gentlemen and whoever wins will share with the other.'

So they shook on it to seal the deal and eventually landed close to the magician's palace. He received them with the honour due to kings. Then he sat them down under a canopy and asked to hear of all their woes.

The brother began by telling how disgracefully he had treated his own sister and how honourably she had behaved in cutting off her hands. He had acted like a dog, locking her in a chest and throwing her to the waves. His conscience was a purgatory of remorse and shame. Even worse, he was grief-stricken by the loss of his good and brave sister. If all the sorrows of the souls in hell were weighed against his, his suffering would be greatest.

When the brother fell silent, the King said, 'Pah! Your pain is nothing compared to my torture. I found a handless maiden in a trunk and she became my beloved wife. She bore me a gorgeous son, but I had them nearly burned alive because of the trickery of an evil fishwife. They were both exiled from my kingdom and now I can have no peace, day or night, and my blood is like knives is my veins.'

After the magician had listened to the two kings, he realised that one was the brother and the other the husband of Penta. So he called for Penta's son and said, 'Kiss the feet of your father.'

The boy obeyed the magician, and the King his father, seeing how gentle and lovely he was, placed a golden chain around his neck.

Then the magician said, 'Kiss the hand of your uncle.'

The boy did as he was asked, swiftly and gracefully, and the uncle, impressed by the boy's manners, gave him a precious ruby and asked the magician if he was his son.

'Ask the mother,' replied the magician.

Penta, who had been concealed behind a curtain, came out in a state of rapture. She ran back and forth between her brother and her husband, feeling the love of family on the one hand and the love of passion on the other. They made a triangle of joy, talking excitedly and laughing, making a kind of human music. Then they pulled the boy into the magic circle and the father and uncle took turns in throwing him in the air with delight. At the end of all this pure joy, the magician spoke:

'Only heaven will know how happy I am to see Queen Penta comforted at last, because she deserves to be cherished for her wonderful qualities. That is why I started this competition in the hope of bringing her husband and her brother here. I will keep the word of my proclamation and I have decided that the Queen's husband has suffered most. He will receive not only the golden crown and sceptre but also my kingdom here. With your agreement, I would like to be a father and grandfather to you all, and you will be as precious to me as my eyes.'

And since he wanted nothing more than to make Penta happy, the magician told her to put her stumps beneath her apron and to keep them there till he asked her to bring them out, when she would have two warm and living hands.

Penta did as he said and it was true and she held her child's face in her hands, which were even more beautiful than before.

Then they were all unbelievably happy for ever, because *until you've tasted bitterness, you do not know what sweetness is.*

Tattercoats

A very wealthy old Lord lived in a great palace by the sea. His wife and children were no longer living, but he had one little granddaughter whom he had never set eyes on since the day she was born. He hated her bitterly because his favourite daughter had died giving birth to her. When the nurse brought him the newborn baby, he raged that he would never look at its face as long as it lived and swore that it could live or die as it liked!

He turned his back and sat by his window staring at the ocean and weeping for his lost daughter and would not move. His white hair and beard grew like sorrow over his shoulders, down his back, twining round his chair and creeping across the floor. His great tears dropped on to the windowsill, and wore away the stone, till they ran away, a salty river of grief, into the sea.

Meanwhile, the little granddaughter grew up with no one to love or care for her or even clothe her properly. Only the old nurse, if no one was around, would give her some leftovers from the kitchen or a torn petticoat from the ragbag. But the other palace servants would force her from the house with pokes and pinches and cruel comments. They called her 'Tattercoats' and jeered at her bare feet, till she ran away crying and hid in the garden.

In this way, Tattercoats grew up, with not much to eat or wear, wandering the fields and meadows with not so much as a pair of shoes. Her only companion was the gooseherd. When she was hungry or cold, he would play to her on his pipe, so merrily that she forgot her troubles. Tattercoats danced to the gooseherd's pipe, with his flock of geese as partners.

One day, the people began to talk excitedly about a splendid ball that the King was giving in the town nearby. The King was travelling the land with his only son, who was to choose a bride and all the lords and ladies of the county were to be invited.

Sure enough, an invitation was delivered to the palace by the sea, and the servants brought it to the old Lord, who still sat by his window, shrouded in his long white hair and weeping into the river that was swollen by his tears.

But when he heard the King's command, he stopped crying and his dried his red eyes. He told his servants to fetch shears to cut him loose, because his hair had tied him up like bereavement's prisoner and he could not move. Then he sent them for his finest clothes and most impressive jewels and dressed in them. He ordered them to put the gold saddle on his white horse so that he could ride out splendidly to meet the King.

Tattercoats had heard all about the exciting events in the town. She sat crying by the kitchen door because she could not go. When the old nurse heard the girl's distress, she went to the Lord and pleaded with him to take his granddaughter to the King's ball.

The old Lord scowled and told her to hold her tongue, while the servants roared with laughter and said: 'Tattercoats is happy in her rags, playing with the goose-herd, and that's all she's fit for!'

A second time, and then a third, the nurse begged the Lord to take the girl to the ball. But she only received black looks and dark words, till she was pushed out of the room by the sneering servants.

In tears by now, the old nurse went looking for Tatter-coats – but the cook had swept Tattercoats away with a broom and she'd run to the gooseherd to tell him how unhappy she was over the King's ball.

The gooseherd listened, then told her to cheer up. He said that they should go together to the town to see the King and all the wonderful things themselves. When Tattercoats looked sadly down at her torn petticoat and her bare feet, he played on his pipe so entertainingly that she felt better at once. The boy took her by the hand and they danced down the road towards the town, with the geese dancing before them.

They hadn't gone very far, when a handsome young man in the finest clothes rode up and asked the way to the castle where the King was staying. When they said that they were going that way, he dismounted and walked beside them along the road.

The gooseherd began to play a low, sweet tune on his pipe. The stranger gazed and gazed at Tattercoats' beautiful face till he fell deeply in love with her and begged her to marry him.

Tattercoats laughed and shook her lovely head.

'You would be disgraced if your wife was a goosegirl! Ask one of the fine ladies you'll meet at the ball and don't tease poor Tattercoats.'

But the more she declined his proposal, the sweeter the pipe played and the deeper the young man fell in love. To prove his sincerity, he asked her to come at midnight to the King's ball, exactly as she was, with the geese and the gooseherd. He would dance with her – rags, bare feet and all – in front of the King and the noblest in the county; then introduce her as his beloved, beautiful bride.

So when night fell, and the castle ballroom was brilliant with light and music, and the lords and ladies pranced before the King, just as the clock struck twelve, Tattercoats, the gooseherd and his flock of noisy geese came in through the great doors and walked up the ballroom. All around them, the ladies whispered and sniggered and the lords scoffed and guffawed, while the King on his throne stared in astonishment. But Tattercoats' lover was seated next to the King and he rose to greet her. Taking her by the hand he kissed her passionately, then turned to the King.

'Father,' he said, for it was the Prince himself, 'I have made my choice and here is my bride – the most beautiful girl in all the land, and the kindest too.'

Before he had finished speaking, the gooseherd began to play a melody on his pipe that sounded as sweet as a bird singing in the woods. As he played, Tattercoats' petticoat was changed to a shining gown sewn with glittering jewels. A tiara gleamed in her hair, and the flock of geese behind her became an escort of elegant pages and bridesmaids, holding her long train.

As the King stood to welcome his new daughter, the trumpets played a fanfare in honour of the Princess, and the people outside in the streets told each other that the Prince had chosen for his wife the most beautiful girl in the land, and the kindest too!

The gooseherd was never seen or heard of again, and to this day no one knows what became of him.

The old Lord clopped home to his palace, because he could not stay at court when he had sworn never to look on his granddaughter's face.

He is still sitting by his window, weeping his bitter tears into the river that runs into the sea.

Invisible

This lad lived happily with his parents on the edge of a village in the very last cottage before the forest began.

His mother worked in the woods collecting chestnuts, hazelnuts and walnuts.

His father laboured as a woodcutter, chopping up wood for furniture and fuel.

But one terrible day the father had an accident in the forest and died. The lad and his mother wept as the father was buried in a coffin nailed together from wood he had cut down himself. They grieved for two winters, but when spring came again, the lad's mother met a new man and married him.

When his mother and stepfather came home from their honeymoon, the lad was waiting for them.

His mother ran to him and kissed him, but his stepfather looked straight through him as though he wasn't there.

When bedtime came, the lad kissed his mother good-night, but when he looked to do the same to his stepfather, the man ignored him and carried on reading his book.

The lad climbed the stairs and lay on his narrow bed. The moon stooped and stared at him through the window with its scarred old face. The lad got up and looked out at the forest where his father had died, where alder, ash, aspen, willow, beech, cherry, poplar, oak, birch, hawthorn, hazel, juniper, lime, rowan, pine, elm and yew whispered in darkness; but his sorrow had hardened now and his tears were small glass stones in his eyes.

The lad slept late and when he came down for breakfast, his mother had already left to collect nuts in the forest.

His stepfather was writing letters at the table and barely glanced at him when he sat down with his milk and his bread roll.

The lad ate in silence, conscious of the small slurps he made as he drank. The air around his stepfather seemed dark and heavy, as though he made his own weather. He was a handsome man, unsmiling and strong. There were black hairs on the back of his hands. The man looked up and the lad jumped, worried that he'd been caught staring. But the stepfather said nothing, took his coat from the back of the kitchen door and went out, banging the door behind him. The lad went to the mirror on the wall and stared at his pale thin face.

A sunny day came and the lad knew there was to be a trip to the travelling fair that was on in the big town. He woke early and washed himself and brushed his hair and got dressed in his favourite clothes. But when he came downstairs, he saw that his mother had been crying. His stepfather walked past him without a word and went outside to wait for his wife by the gate. The mother couldn't look her son in the eyes.

She pressed some coins into his palm and told him that he wasn't to come to the fair, but was to stay behind and buy himself some lunch from the village shop. They would be back late, she said, and he was to be in bed when they returned.

Her son shouted at her and chucked the coins at her feet, but she shook her head and hurried to the gate to join her husband. The lad left the coins glinting on the floor and promised himself that he would go hungry rather than spend them. He stuffed his pockets with nuts from his mother's collecting basket and ran to the woods.

Dusk came and the forest sulked and darkened. The lad grew cold and climbed down from the branch he'd been sitting on. He made his way back along the path, passing the stumps of trees cut down by his dead father. There was no one at home. He ate some fruit from the bowl, then went up to bed. Hours later, the noise of his mother and stepfather returning to the cottage woke him. His door was ajar and he saw them go past on the way to their bedroom. The lamp on the landing lit up their faces, but they did not look in his room.

The days and weeks and months went on till spring, summer and autumn were gone and it was winter again. The lad moved round the house like a ghost and if ever he caught his mother's eye she looked away. He had stopped going to school, but nobody seemed to notice; and when his stepfather met the schoolteacher in the village inn, nothing was said.

One day, the lad came into the kitchen for an apple and saw his stepfather standing there. The lad reached for the apple in the bowl but as he did so the stepfather's big hand swooped down and seized it. He looked into the man's eyes and heard the crunch as he bit into the apple, but the man strolled past him, brushing against him as though he was air, as though he was nothing.

The lad went to the mirror again, but when he gazed there he could only see the reflection of the kitchen – his mother's empty collecting basket on the table, the man's heavy coat hanging on the hook of the door. He leaned closer to the mirror and breathed, but the glass stayed as bright and clear as before. He pressed the flat palm of his hand against it, but although he could feel the coldness of the mirror he could see nothing of himself.

Terrified, with his heart jerking in his chest, the lad ran upstairs to his mother's bedroom. He sat down at the stool in front of the dressing table and stared wildly into each of the three mirrors there. His face was in none of them.

He fled downstairs and into the sitting room where his mother and stepfather sat. In her arms, his mother held a new baby, carefully wrapped in a soft white blanket. He called his mother's name, but she bent low over the baby's head and made a shushing sound. The stepfather stood up and walked towards him, tall and brooding.

The lad backed away before him and the man shut the door in his face.

And now the lad was truly invisible. He had grown in the year since his mother had married again and his clothes were tight-fitting or too short. Since no one could see him, he put on a big old shirt of his father's and went about in that. He left home in the morning and spent his days in the forest.

In the evenings, he returned to the cottage, taking some food – bread or fruit or nuts – up to his room and eating it there. Sometimes he stood at the side of the baby's crib and looked down at his half-brother, but he was always quiet as he knew the child could not see him.

If he passed his mother in the house, she busied herself at something, or buried her face in her baby's neck. To his stepfather, he was less than a shadow on the stairs. At night he lay alone on his bed, hearing his mother cry and the man shout.

Time passed. One day, as he walked in the woods, the young man, who was tall now and broad-shouldered, saw a girl of his own age sitting on the branch of his favourite tree and swinging her legs. So used was he to being invisible, that he stood and stared at her from the path. But the girl turned her bright hazel eyes on his and laughed at him.

Then she reached into the dense foliage of the tree, rustled there, and tossed him the shiniest, reddest apple in the world. He caught it low with his left hand, like a catch at cricket. Then he remembered that he had on only his father's old shirt, which came to his knees, so he turned and ran away into the forest, clutching the apple. But the girl jumped down from the tree and chased him, and as she was a faster runner than the young man, she soon caught up with him, and she grabbed him by his shirt-tail and kissed him on the lips.

When he woke the next morning, the young man climbed up to the small attic and found the chest which contained his dead father's things.

He put on some soft corduroy trousers, a clean linen shirt and a beautiful leather jacket which still held the scent of wood shavings and pine. He took out his father's watch, set it to the right time and put it on his wrist. He pulled on warm socks and good boots.

He went downstairs to the kitchen, where his mother was preparing breakfast. She stared at him and tears scalded her eyes and he knew that she saw him. But the girl from the woods was waiting by the gate and he went out to meet her.

He came home late, under the light of stars that had taken years to arrive, and went to his bed. In the morning, he went off with the girl again, and he felt his mother drink him in with her eyes as she watched him go.

After a month and a day of this, he arrived home one night and found his stepfather in the kitchen. The man looked older and smaller now that the young man had grown so tall and fit, and his black hair was greying. He shouted to the young man that he needn't think he could come and go as he pleased, and with a shock the young man realised that the man was looking at him at last. But he pushed his stepfather easily away and went up to his bed. As he lay there, he heard the man's yells and his mother's wails. Outside his window, the moon scudded high up in the clouds, like a coin tossed for heads or tails.

The next day, the son woke early and for the first time made breakfast for his mother and her child and himself. As they were eating, the stepfather came in, but the son didn't glance at him and eventually the man went awkwardly away.

That night, when the young man came home, he brought the girl with him and cooked a meal for them all, so that she could meet his mother and her child.

The stepfather came in again, just as the son was slicing up a pie, but the son ignored him until the man muttered to himself and disappeared.

Every morning, the young man rose early to prepare breakfast and each night he came home with the girl and cooked supper. He worked in the forest now, chopping wood as his father had done.

When the girl looked at him, she had love in her hazel eyes, like a light, and as it shone on him he grew stronger and more handsome.

The mother stared at her two sons and began to notice all the ways in which they were alike. There was no more shouting or crying in the house and the son resolutely treated his stepfather as though he was invisible.

The sullen man kept to himself and bothered nobody. One day he vanished altogether, taking his coat from the hook on the back of the door, and it was as though he had never been there at all. The young man worked hard in the forest to keep food on the table for the family and the girl took the collecting basket from the mother to gather chestnuts, hazelnuts and walnuts.

They were all very happy and as his small half-brother grew, the young man made sure to watch over him, with the light of love in his eyes.

Nine Words

A long time ago – before the invention of writing or even sign language – there was a Prince who was put under a curse by a wicked witch. He had done nothing wrong, but her evil spell was that the Prince could only speak one word each year. He was permitted to save up the words, though – so that if he kept shtum for a whole year then the next year he could speak two words, and so on and so forth.

One day he met a beautiful Princess and fell madly in love with her, body and soul. With almost superhuman effort he set out not to speak for two whole years so that he could take her hand, look at her and say, 'My darling.' But at the end of the two years he wanted to tell her that he loved her. So he waited another three long years without uttering a peep. This brought the number of dumb years to five.

At the end of five years, he knew that he just had to ask her to marry him. So he bit his lip and endured another one, two, three, four years in total silence.

At last, as the ninth year of wordlessness ended, he took the lovely Princess to the most private and romantic spot in the royal garden and heaped a hundred red roses into her lap. Then he knelt before her, took her hand, looked into her eyes and croaked out in a hoarse voice:

'My darling! I love you! Will you marry me?'

And the Princess tidied a strand of her soft hair behind the most beautiful of ears, opened her dreamy eyes wide, parted her soft pink lips and said, 'Pardon?'

Wooden Maria

A King and his wife had a beautiful only daughter, Maria. When Maria was fifteen, her beloved mother became fatally ill and there was nothing to be done. Maria's father knelt sobbing at the Queen's bedside and vowed that he would never marry again. But his wife hushed him tenderly. 'I must die,' she said. 'But you have our daughter to raise. I am leaving you this ring. You must promise to marry the woman whose finger fits the ring.'

The bleak mourning-time passed and the King began to search for a new wife. He went from one woman to another, but the ring was too big for half of them and too small for the rest. He was secretly relieved and decided to leave things as they were for now.

But one day Maria was rummaging through her mother's things and she found the ring at the back of a drawer. She tried it on and couldn't get it off. 'What will Father say?' she wondered. So she wrapped a bandage round her finger and when her father noticed she said she had cut her finger. He insisted on taking a look, undid the bandage and there was the ring! 'Oh my goodness, Maria!' he exclaimed. 'I will have to marry *you*!'

Maria was shocked and laughed and cried at the same time. 'I can't be your wife! I'm your daughter!'

But the King was adamant he must keep to his promise and Maria went along with it on condition he bring her a dress the colour of meadows and all the flowers in the world; another dress the colour of the sea with every fish in it; and a bridal gown the colour of the sun, the moon and all the stars. She reckoned she was demanding the impossible, but after six months of searching, her father presented her with the three gowns, each one in its own way the most amazing that could be imagined.

'One thing more,' said Maria.

'What else could you possibly wish for?' said her father.

'I want another dress, made of wood.'

The King immediately had a wooden dress made and for the first time in ages, Maria seemed pleased.

On the day of the wedding, she put on the three gorgeous dresses, then the wooden dress on top, and set off for the river. She pretended to bathe, then threw herself in; but instead of sinking and drowning, she floated away, down the river, out to sea, bobbing over the waves, on and on, until she came to a place where a King's son was fishing.

'I've never seen a fish like that,' he thought, and he spread his net and pulled her on to dry land.

'Who are you and where are you from?' he asked.

'I am Wooden Maria and I go where the water takes me.'

'Why are you dressed in wood? Why do you float without drowning?'

She told him that she was a poor girl who had only a wooden dress that floated like a boat, and that she wanted to be of service.

'What can you do?'

'Everything and nothing.'

This amused him so he took her to his castle and hired her as a rat-catcher for the rats were forever plundering the eggs from the geese. Instead of setting traps for the rats, Maria whistled and sang jolly tunes and tapped out the rhythms on her wooden dress so that soon enough the rats became her pets and danced around her. She fed them on scraps from the kitchen and the rats left the geese and their eggs in peace.

Every evening, Wooden Maria returned to the castle with a basket of eggs and one evening she found the King's son getting ready to go to the ball.

'Where are you off to, heir to the King?'

'Mind your own business, wooden thing!'

'Take me dancing to the ball?'

'You don't have a chance at all!'

Maria grew quiet, but when she was alone she put on the dress the colour of meadows and all the flowers in the world and became the most beautiful woman that was ever seen. At the ball, she sat near the King's son. He asked her at once to dance and would dance with no one else. He fell head over heels in love with her and gave her the gold pin from his lapel.

'Who are you and where are you from?' he asked.

'I am the Countess Thwartscoff,' she replied, but no one there knew her at all. Before the ball was over, she disappeared and the King's son could not find her. She hurried home and put on her wooden dress.

The following evening, he dressed again for the ball and Wooden Maria said to him:

'Your Highness, take me as your guest.'

'Not in that ugly wooden dress!'

'Take me dancing! Please be kind!'

'Silence! I have something on my mind.'

And he grew angry and threatened her with a stick.

After he'd gone, Maria put on the dress the colour of the sea with every fish in it. When she arrived at the ball, the guests gaped because they had never seen someone so beautiful. The men formed a queue to ask her to dance, but she would say yes only to the King's son.

'Who are you and where are you from?' he beseeched.

'I am the Duchess Thwartstick,' was all she would say. The King's son was besotted and gave her the diamond ring from his pinkie. They danced and danced then suddenly she disappeared and the smitten Prince ran everywhere but no one could tell him where she had gone.

The next evening as he prepared for the ball, he was in an agony of hope and despair. Wooden Maria came up to him but he was in no mood for her rat-catcher's cheek and

93

he shoved her away. At the ball, her beauty was dazzling, for she wore the gown the colour of the sun, the moon and all the stars. The King's son gave her the locket from round his neck which held his portrait.

'Who are you and where do you come from?' he begged.

He knelt enraptured at her feet as she told him she was Princess Thwartshove, and the next moment she had given him the slip.

The King's son was struck down with love-sickness and took to his bed. Each day he grew worse, asking everyone over and over if they knew anything about the beautiful girl and swearing he would die unless he saw her again. The whole castle thought he was bonkers. Wooden Maria heard everything and said nothing.

One day, when the King's son was more dead than alive, she slipped something in the soup the son was to sup. Not a soul saw her and the butler took him the soup. He managed a spoonful but something sharp stuck in his throat and he coughed it up. It was the golden pin he had given to the gorgeous Countess!

'Who made this soup?' he gasped.

'The cook made it,' said the butler.

'Well, I can't eat it. Bring me something else immediately.'

The cook was put out and asked the rat-catcher girl to fetch eggs for an omelette. But when he turned his back, she dropped the diamond ring into the mixture. The King's son took a bite of the omelette and nearly broke a tooth on the diamond. Then he ordered that Wooden Maria was to make him a pie. The cook, the butler and the rest of the staff complained about this loopy behaviour, but the pie was made and dished up soon enough. When the pining Prince forked out the locket with his portrait, he ran down to the yard.

There he found the rats dancing around the girl in the wooden dress, singing:

'She dresses in wood
And loves who she should!'

Then Maria told him her story from beginning to end and before anyone knew it they were hand in glove and deep in love and wife and man and King and Queen, through tears and laughter, happy ever after.

The Squire's Bride

This rich Squire owned a dirty great manor and had loads of gold stashed in his chest and plenty more coming in from money-lending. But something was missing, because he was a widower. The young lass from the nearby farm worked for him and he'd taken a right shine to her. Her family was hard up and he reckoned that if he so much as hinted or winked at matrimony she'd be all over him like a rash. So he told her that he had hit upon the notion of getting wed again.

'Ooh! It's surprising what one can hit upon!' said the girl, standing there giggling. She reckoned the revolting old goat should've hit upon something else!

'Well, I have hit upon the idea that *you* should be my new wife!' said the Squire.

The young girl replied prettily, 'Thanks, but no thanks!' and thought, 'That day will be a long time coming, Squire!'

Of course, the less she wanted him, the more he wanted her and he wasn't used to taking no for an answer. He got nowhere with the lass, so he sent for her father. If the father could fix him up with the girl, he could forget about the money he owed him and the Squire would throw in that piece of land next to his field on top.

The father thought his daughter was only a child who didn't know what was best for her. Yes, he promised the Squire, he'd sort it, no problem.

But his daughter would have none of it, whether he yelled or wheedled. She wouldn't marry the Squire if he sat in powdered gold from arsehole to earhole, so there!

The Squire waited for news, day and night, but no, nowt. At last, angry and impatient, he told the father he couldn't wait any longer. If the father was to keep his promise, he must settle matters at once.

The father told the Squire to get everything ready for the wedding and when the parson and all the guests were assembled, he was to send for the girl on a work pretext. When she arrived, she must be spliced in a trice, before she knew what was to do.

'Good plan, good plan,' said the smitten Squire. So he had his servants brew and bake like maniacs, had a wedding cake made and a wedding punch assembled. And when everyone arrived in their finery for the feast the Squire told one of his lads to run down to the farm and have the father send up what he'd promised. He shook his fist at the lad and told him to be back in the pop of a cork or he'd get what for, so the lad legged it.

'I've come from the Squire to fetch what you promised him,' he said to the father. 'But it has to be this instant because he's in a right old state today.'

'No problem! No problem! Get down to the field and take her with you. You'll see her there.'

The boy rushed to the field and saw the daughter raking there. 'I'm to take what your father promised the Squire,' he said.

The girl wasn't daft. 'Is that right?' she said. 'It's the little white mare over there by the cabbages. Take her away.'

The lad jumped on to the little mare's back and galloped home at full pelt.

'Did you get her?' asked the Squire.

'She's standing by the front door,' replied the lad.

'Well, take her up to Mother's bedroom!' said the Squire.

'Bloody hell! How's that to be managed?' said the lad.

The Squire thought he meant the girl might kick up a fuss. 'Do as I say,' he said, 'and if you can't manage her on your own, get the others to help you.'

The Squire was puce in the face, so the lad got all the servants together and some hauled on the front half and some shoved on the back, and at last they got the mare up the stairs and into the bedroom. The wedding dress, veil, gloves and so on were all laid out for the Squire's bride.

'I've taken her upstairs, Squire,' said the lad. 'But it was the worst job I've had since I started work here.'

'It'll be worth it,' said the Squire. 'Now send some women up to dress her.'

'Bloody hell! How's that to be done?' said the lad.

'None of your lip! They're to get her dressed and to forget neither garter nor garland,' snapped the Squire.

The lad went to the kitchen. 'Listen, girls,' he said, 'get yourselves upstairs and dress that little mare as a bride. The Squire must want to give his guests a good laugh.'

So the housemaids put the bridal outfit on the mare and the lad went to the Squire to tell him she was ready, and wearing both garter and garland.

'Tickety-boo!' said the Squire. 'Bring her down and I'll greet her at the door myself.'

There was an almighty clattering on the stairs and the sound of snorting and neighing. Then the door opened, the Squire's bride came into the great hall, and all the wedding guests fell about laughing.

And it must have been a very happy union, because they reckon the Squire hasn't gone courting since!

The Lost Happy Endings

The Rat's job was important. Each evening when dusk was removing the outlines of things, like a rubber, the Rat had to shoulder his sack and carry all the Happy Endings of stories from one end of the forest to the other, in time for everybody's bedtime. Then the Rat had to climb on to the branch of the ancient oak tree, open the sack and shake out the Happy Endings into the darkening air.

Some of the Endings drifted away like breath and others fluttered upwards like moths fumbling for light. Some looked like fireflies disappearing among the kindling of the leaves and twigs and some were fireworks, zipping skywards like rockets and flouncing off in a jackpot of sparks high above the forest.

When the last Ending was out of the sack, the Rat would scamper and rustle his way homewards through the woods. Sometimes the eyes of owls flashed from the trees like torches and made him jump, or bats skimmed the top of his head like living frisbees and he squeaked with surprise; but the Rat ran speedily along and was soon home in his hole.

He would sleep quite late the following day. By the time he'd washed, eaten and visited other rats down by the river, the Happy Endings had flown back to the forest like homing pigeons and were hanging from the old silver birch all ready for the Rat to collect once more.

One evening, as the Rat set off with his sack, he noticed scarves of mist draped in the trees. One of them noosed itself round the Rat's neck, soft and damp, and made him shiver.

By the time he had reached the middle of the forest, the mist had thickened and the Rat could only see a little way ahead. The shadowy trees looked villainous: tall ghouls with long arms and twiggy fingers. Bushes crouched in the fog as though they might pounce like muggers. The Rat hurried on.

'Hello, my verminous deario!'

The Rat jumped. A twisted old witch with a face like the bark of a tree and horrible claw hands was standing on the path in front of the Rat. She had fierce red eyes like poisonous berries.

'What's in the sack?'

'Let me pass,' said the Rat.

'What's in the sack, I said!'

The witch had grabbed hold of the Rat's tail. Her touch nipped like pepper.

'Let me alone!' gasped the Rat. 'I must go on.'

'Shut up, rodent!' said the vicious witch, and she spat green spittle in the Rat's face. The Rat was so shocked that he jumped backwards and rolled over a tree root. Faster than fury, the witch was on him and had snatched the sack of Happy Endings.

'I'm having this, my rat-faced deario,' she snarled. Then she gobbed at the Rat again and hobbled rapidly away into the darkness and the fog. The Rat cowered for a long time, terrified that the witch would return.

The fog began to lift and the moon turned the narrow path through the forest to a long silver finger. An owl's hoot questioned sadly. The Rat looked about. The Happy Endings were lost! He turned and ran back down the path to his home, scattering bitter tears into the cold black night.

As the Rat ran crying through the forest, children in their beds were listening to their bedtime stories. But to-night there were to be no Happy Endings.

Wooden Maria sank to the bottom of the sea and she drowned. The children started to cry.

The lass who worked on the farm was forced to marry the old squire and scrub him in the bath before bed. The children started to scream.

The children of Hamelin, trapped inside the mountain, ate each other or starved to death. The children had hysterics.

On and on the parents of the children read, and worse and worse the tales became. Soon the night was filled with the awful sound of frightened and traumatised children weeping and wailing in their beds.

There was a cacophony of children crying or asking for the light to be left on or refusing to sleep alone or wetting the bed. The Rat rocked back and forth moaning with sorrow.

When dawn came, it grew quieter, and the exhausted Rat fell fast asleep. As he slept, he dreamed of a Golden Pen which could write on night itself . . .

He seized the pen and set off into the forest. It grew dark. Stars whispered.

The Rat dreamed that he came to the spot where the witch had snitched his sack.

Wondering what to do, he held the Golden Pen and drew a question mark on the night air. It floated before him, glowing in the darkness.

Suddenly the Rat knew exactly what to do. He would write his own Happy Ending on the night! He wrote in the air and every word shone out in perfect golden handwriting:

'When the witch first opened the sack of Happy Endings she was furious. Worthless to a witch. Boring. Stupid.

'She flung the sack into the corner of her lair and went out to bite the head off any small songbird she could catch and crunch its beak. It was good to be bad. Then she decided to burn the sack of Happy Endings. She would dance around the fire and shout out terrible swear words and drink poison-berry juice and smoke a clay pipe. Good to be bad.

'So she lugged the sack outside, added a few dried leaves and twigs, then squatted down and began to rub two sticks together to light the fire.

'The rapid movement of her witchy hands made a spark, then another, and another, and soon the fire was born. Suddenly a spark leapt from the stick and jumped on to a lock of her frizzy old hair. There was a nasty burny hairy smell and – whumph! The Witch's hair was alight.

'She shrieked horribly, beating at her head with her hands. She danced crazily around the fire, singing hideously. The flames danced with her, cheek to cheek, step by step, arm in arm, one-two-three, one-two-three. Her screams scattered the sleeping birds from the trees in a panic of wings.'

The Rat heard an awful noise and smelled something strange cooking. He followed his nose and it led him to the bowels of the forest. The fire opened its jaws and roared.

He stared in horror into the Witch's small red eyes until they were burned completely black and the Witch collapsed in a sullen hiss of ash . . .

He saw the sack on the ground.

The sack of Happy Endings!

There was still time, if he ran as fast as he ever had in his life, to send the Happy Endings out into the world.

Goosegirls went to the ball and grooms lived happily ever after . . .

Squires with little taste and loads of cash produced as much food as a peasant could ever wish for and . . . Look! Look! Look! Lost children were running home through the woods into the arms of their parents.